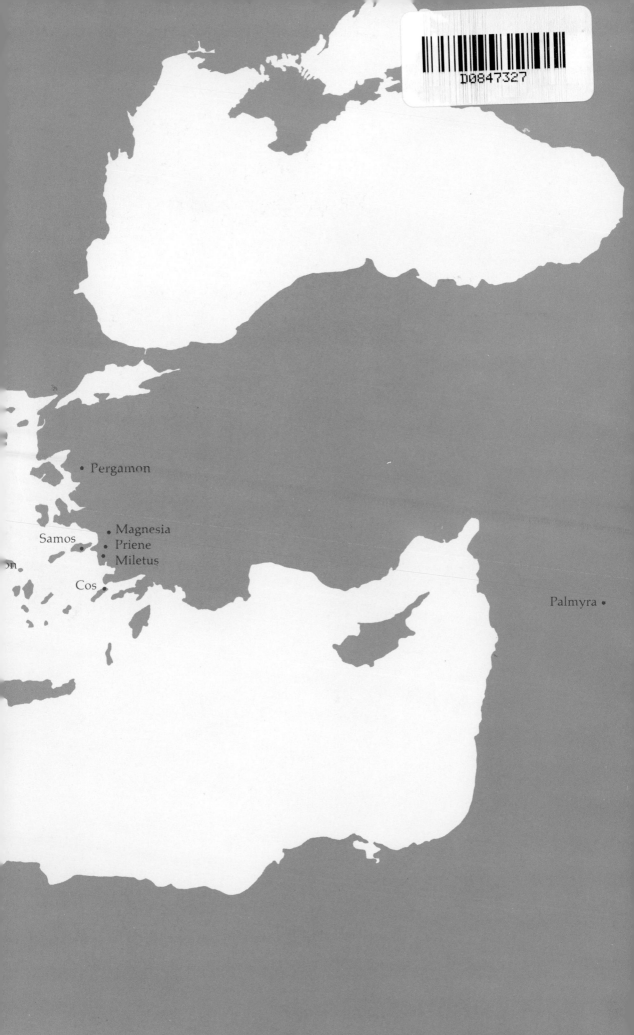

Pergamon

Magnesia
Samos
Priene
Miletus

Cos

Palmyra

Architectural Space
in Ancient Greece

The MIT Press
Cambridge, Massachusetts, and London, England

Architectural Space
in Ancient Greece

C. A. Doxiadis

Translated and Edited by Jaqueline Tyrwhitt

Originally published in German in 1937 under the
title *Raumordnung im griechischen Städtebau.* Translated
with permission of Kurt Vowinckel Verlag,
Heidelberg

This book was designed by The MIT Press Design
Department. It was set in Fototronic Elegante by
York Graphic Services, Inc., printed on Warren's
Old Style by Halliday Lithograph Corp., and bound
in G. S. B. Bookcloth by Halliday Lithograph Corp.
in the United States of America.

ISBN 0 262 04021 2 (hardcover)

Library of Congress catalog card number: 74-87300

To the memory of my father and mother

Contents

Editor's Note

In Chapters 5, 6, 7, notes and references are placed at the end of each site description rather than at the end of the chapter. Notes added for this edition are in brackets. Works consulted for the purpose of this edition appear in the bibliographical lists under the heading "Additional References."

Abbreviations Used in the Bibliographies

AbhPreuss.
Preussische Akademie der Wissenschaften. *Abhandlungen. Philosophisch-Historische Klasse.*

AJA
American Journal of Archaeology

Ath Mitt.
Deutsches Archäologisches Institut. *Mitteilungen. Athenische Abteilung.*

BCH
Bulletin de correspondance hellénique

BSA
British School at Athens. *Annual.*

Preface

This is the first translation into English of my doctoral dissertation, which was prepared at the Berlin Charlottenburg Technische Hochschule and published in 1937 as *Raumordnung im griechischen Städtebau*.

My preface to the original edition began as follows:

Two great advances of the last three decades have radically altered the conditions that prevailed in cities over the last three millennia. The first advance concerns building materials. Until about the beginning of this century, man built with clay and stone, wood and marble, natural materials whose characteristic properties of weight and size determined the scale and form of the buildings. Today, the increasing industrialized production of new building materials has given man the freedom to create structures of whatever scale and form he may desire. The second advance concerns transportation. Until the last century man could proceed beyond the pedestrian range only with the help of animals. Today mechanized transportation reigns supreme and is completely altering the form and scale of our cities.

The problems caused by these changing conditions made me determined to discover what man might hold onto in a situation where city planning policies could "as easily lead to terrible failures as to happy solutions" for mankind. I determined to discover what was "the human scale"; what was the secret of the system of architectural spacing used by the ancient Greeks, which had the effect of satisfying man and uplifting his spirit as he entered a public space— whether it was a precinct sacred to the gods with its temples and votive columns or the agora with its stoas and statuary. As a student in Athens, I had visited and studied all the best-known archaeological sites in Greece and, later, several in Asia Minor. In Berlin I was able to restudy them and compare my findings with those of several outstanding archaeologists, including my professor, Dr. Daniel Krencker, Dr. Wilhelm Dörpfeld, Dr. Theodor Wiegand, then President of the German Archaeological Institute, and many other scholars from the various national archaeological schools and institutes in Athens.

The text of this edition does not constitute a major revision of the original, although some sections have been rearranged, minor inaccuracies have been corrected, and additional references and new illustrations have been provided. The sites discussed in this book thus include only those that had been fully excavated and documented before 1936, when my thesis was written, and their state of preservation as described here is that in which I found them at that time. There has, of course, been a considerable change in the number and condition of the excavated sites in the last thirty years. In cases where findings made since 1936 have altered the situation as I have described it, reference to these is given in the notes. At the Heraion at Samos, for example, excavations are still proceeding. Here I had postulated the position of an entry based on the theory of polar coordinates. Recent findings on the site have shown the existence of an entry close to the point I had selected but not close enough to be conclusive.

Of the sites necessarily omitted from my 1936 study the best known are perhaps Delos and Corinth, but there are also many minor sites, such as Perachora, Kea, Vraona, awaiting investigations that will throw further light on the theory I put forward here.

To Professor Jaqueline Tyrwhitt I express my gratitude for her translation of my German text and for her supervision of this English edition. I acknowledge also the contribution of my young colleague Andreas Drymiotis, engineer-mathematician, who found the time to take some new photographs of the ancient sites. His photographs add to the quality of this presentation.

Constantinos A. Doxiadis
Athens, 1969

Illustrations

Unless otherwise noted, illustrations are by
C. A. Doxiadis. Page numbers are in brackets.

1 [35]
Athens, Acropolis. View from point A, 1968.
(Photo: A. Drymiotis.)

2 [35]
Athens, Acropolis III, after 450 B.C. Perspective
from point A.

3 [36]
Athens, Acropolis I, circa 530 B.C. Plan.

4 [36]
Athens, Acropolis II, circa 480 B.C. Plan.

5 [37]
Athens, Acropolis III, after 450 B.C. Plan.

6 [38]
Athens, Acropolis II and III. Plan (W. B. Dins-
moor, *The Architecture of Ancient Greece*, London:
Batsford, 1950, fig. 74.)

7 [41]
Delphi, Terrace of Apollo. View from point C,
1968. (Photo: A. Drymiotis.)

8 [42]
Delphi, Terrace of Apollo. Plan of temple.

9 [42]
Delphi, Terrace of Apollo. Elevation of temple
and terrace. (Fernand Courby, *La Terrasse du
temple*, pt. 1, Fouilles de Delphes, vol. 2, Paris:
De Boccard, 1927, fig. 157.)

10 [43]
Delphi, Terrace of Apollo. View from point B,
1968. (Photo: A. Drymiotis.)

11 [44]
Delphi, Terrace of Apollo. Monument to
Eumenes II. (Fernand Courby, *La Terrasse du
temple*, pt. 1, Fouilles de Delphes, vol. 2, Paris:
De Boccard, 1927, fig. 221.)

12 [44]
Delphi, Terrace of Apollo. Monument to
Aemilius Paullus. (Heinz Kähler, *Der Fries vom
Reiterdenkmal des Aemilius Paullus in Delphi*, Berlin:
Mann, 1965.)

13 [45]
Delphi, Terrace of Apollo. Restoration. (Albert
Tournaire, *Relevés et restaurations*, pt. 1, Fouilles
de Delphes, vol. 2, Paris: Fontemoing, 1902, pl.
6.)

14 [45]
Delphi, Terrace of Apollo. Sketch showing view
from the southwest in ancient times.

15 [46]
Delphi. General plan of sacred precinct.
(H. Pomtow, "Delphoi: Die Topographie," in
A. F. von Pauly, ed., *Real-Encyclopädie der classischen
Altertumswissenschaft*, suppl. 4, Stuttgart: Metzler,
1924, p. 1199.)

16 [47]
Delphi. General plan of sacred precinct. (Pierre
de la Coste-Messelière, *Delphes*, Paris: Editions
du Chêne, 1943.

17 [50]
Aegina, Sacred Precinct of Aphaia. View from
point A, 1968. (Photo: A. Drymiotis.)

18 [51]
Aegina, Sacred Precinct of Aphaia. View
(drawn in 1901). (Adolph Furtwängler, *Aegina:
das Heiligtum der Aphaia*, Munich: Franz, 1906,
pl. 2.)

19 [52]
Aegina, Sacred Precinct of Aphaia, early fifth
century B.C. Plan.

20 [53]
Aegina, Sacred Precinct of Aphaia. Plan, showing four different periods. (Adolf Furtwängler,
Aegina: das Heiligtum der Aphaia, Munich: Franz,
1906, suppl. 5.)

21 [53]
Aegina, Sacred Precinct of Aphaia. Plan of the
great altar. (Adolf Furtwängler, *Aegina: das Heiligtum der Aphaia*, Munich: Franz, 1906, fig. 22.)

22 [57]
Miletus, Delphineion. View from the west,
circa 1914. (Georg Kawerau and Albert Rehm,
Das Delphinion in Milet, Berlin, Staatliche
Museen, Milet: Ergebnisse der Ausgrabungen
und Untersuchungen seit dem Jahre 1899, ed.
Theodor Wiegand, vol. 1, pt. 3, Berlin: Reimer,
1914, pl. 6.)

23 [57]
Miletus, Delphineion I, fifth and fourth centuries B.C. Plan.

24 [58]
Miletus, Delphineion II, third and second centuries B.C. Plan.

25 [58]
Miletus, Delphineion II. Plan of detail.

26 [59]
Miletus, Delphineion III, first century B.C. and
first century A.D. Plan.

27 [60]
Miletus, Delphineion IV, after first century A.D.
Plan.

28 [61]
Miletus, Delphineion III. Reconstruction.
(Georg Kawerau and Albert Rehm, *Das Del-
phinion in Milet*, Berlin, Staatliche Museen,
Milet: Ergebnisse der Augsgrabungen und
Untersuchungen seit dem Jahre 1899, ed.

Theodor Wiegand, vol. 1, pt. 3, Berlin: Reimer, 1914, pl. 4.)

29 [61]
Miletus, Delphineion. Composite plan. (Georg Kawerau and Albert Rehm, *Das Delphinion in Milet*, Berlin, Staatliche Museen, Milet: Ergebnisse der Ausgrabungen und Untersuchungen seit dem Jahre 1899, ed. Theodor Wiegand, vol. 1, pt. 3, Berlin: Reimer, 1914, pl. 7)

30 [64]
Miletus, Agora III. Perspective. (Armin von Gerkan, *Der Nordmarkt und der Hafen an der Löwenbucht*, Berlin, Staatliche Museen, Milet: Ergebnisse der Ausgrabungen und Untersuchungen seit dem Jahre 1899, ed. Theodor Wiegand, vol. 1, pt. 6, Berlin: Reimer, 1922, pl. 27.)

31 [65]
Miletus, Agora I, fifth and fourth centuries B.C. Plan.

32 [66]
Miletus, Agora II, second century B.C. Plan.

33 [67]
Miletus. General plan. (Armin von Gerkan, *Griechische Städtanlagen*, Berlin: De Gruyter, 1924, fig. 6.)

34 [67]
Miletus. Plan of city center. (Armin von Gerkan, *Der Nordmarkt und der Hafen an der Löwenbucht*, Berlin, Staatliche Museen, Milet: Ergebnisse der Ausgrabungen und Untersuchungen seit dem Jahre 1899, ed. Theodor Wiegand, vol. 1, pt. 6, Berlin: Reimer, 1922, fig.1.)

35 [68]
Miletus, Agora III, first century B.C. and first century A.D. Plan.

36 [69]
Miletus, Agora IV, second century A.D. Plan.

37 [70]
Miletus, Agora IV. Perspective. (Armin von Gerkan, *Der Nordmarkt und der Hagen an der Löwenbucht*, Berlin, Staatliche Museen, Milet: Ergebnisse der Ausgrabungen und Untersuchungen Seit dem Jahre 1899, ed. Theodor Wiegand, vol. 1, pt. 6, Berlin: Reimer, 1922, pl. 28.)

38 [78–79]
Olympia, Altis. View from point A, 1969. (Photo: A. Drymiotis.)

39 [80]
Olympia, Altis, Hellenistic period. Plan.

40 [81]
Olympia, Altis. Perspective from point A.

41 [82]
Olympia, Altis. General plan of the Altis and its environment. (Ernst Curtius and Friedrich Adler, eds., *Olympia: die Ergebnisse der von dem deutschen Reich veranstalteten Ausgrabung*, Berlin: Asher, 1897, map 2.

42 [83]
Olympia, Altis. View from a point east of the treasuries, looking south, 1968. (Photo: A. Drymiotis.)

43 [84]
Olympia, Altis. Hellenistic period. Plan.

44 [85]
Olympia, Altis, Hellenistic period. Plan. (Essen, Ausstellung, 1960. *Olympia in der Antike*, Essen, 1960.)

45 [86–87]
Olympia, Altis. View from point B, 1969. (Photo: A. Drymiotis.)

46 [87]
Olympia, Altis. Perspective from point B.

47 [88]
Olympia, Altis. View from point C, 1969. (Photo: A. Drymiotis.)

48 [89]
Olympia, Altis. Perspective from point C.

49 [90]
Olympia, Altis, Roman period. Plan.

50 [91]
Olympia, Altis. Model. (By Hans Schleif, in Wilhelm Dörpfeld, *Alt-Olympia*, Berlin: Mittler, 1935, vol. 2, pl. 1.)

51 [94–95]
Sounion, Sacred Precinct of Poseidon. View from point A, 1969. (Photo: A. Drymiotis.)

52 [96]
Sounion, Sacred Precinct of Poseidon. Plan.

53 [97]
Sounion, Sacred Precinct of Poseidon. General plan. (Valerios Staïs, Τό Σούνιον καί οἱ ναοί Ποσειδῶνος καί 'Αθηνᾶς, Athens: Library of the Archaeological Service, 1920, end paper.)

54 [97]
Sounion, Sacred Precinct of Poseidon. View of temple. (William H. Plommer, "Three Attic Temples," pt. 2, "The Temple of Poseidon," *Annual of the British School at Athens* 45, 1950, pl. 8.)

55 [99]
Pergamon, Agora. View from point A to the west, 1936.

56 [100]
Pergamon, Agora. Plan.

57 [101]
Pergamon. General plan. (Alexander Conze et al., *Stadt und Landschaft*, Berlin, Staatliche

Museen, Die Altertümer von Pergamon, vol. 1, Berlin: Reimer, 1913, pl. 1.)

58 [102]
Pergamon, Agora. Sections. (Jakob Schrammen, *Der grosse Altar; der obere Markt*, Berlin, Staatliche Museen, Die Altertümer von Pergamon, vol. 3, pt. 1, Berlin: Reimer, 1906, pl. 25.)

59 [103]
Pergamon, Agora. General plan. (Jakob Schrammen, *Der grosse Altar; der obere Markt*, Berlin, Staatliche Museen, Die Altertümer von Pergamon, vol. 3, pt. 1, Berlin: Reimer, 1906, pl. 32.)

60 [106]
Pergamon, Sacred Precinct of Athena. Perspective from point A.

61 [107]
Pergamon, Sacred Precinct of Athena. Plan.

62 [108]
Pergamon, Sacred Precinct of Athena. Plan. (Richard Bohn, *Das Heiligtum der Athena Polias Nikephoros*, Berlin, Staatliche Museen, Die Altertümer von Pergamon, vol. 2, Berlin: Spemann, 1885, pl. 40.)

63 [109]
Pergamon, Sacred Precinct of Athena. Reconstruction, seen from the south. (Richard Bohn, *Das Heiligtum der Athena Polias Nikephoros*, Berlin, Staatliche Museen, Die Altertümer von Pergamon, vol. 2, Berlin: Spemann, 1885, pl. 41.)

64 [111]
Pergamon, Altar of Zeus. Plan.

65 [112]
Pergamon, Altar of Zeus and Agora. Plan. (Jakob Schrammen, *Der Grosse Altar; der obere Markt*, Berlin, Staatliche Museen, Die Altertümer von Pergamon, vol. 3, pt. 1, Berlin: Reimer, 1906, pl. 1.)

66 [113]
Pergamon, Altar of Zeus. Reconstruction. (Jakob Schrammen, *Der grosse Altar; der obere Markt*, Berlin, Staatliche Museen, Die Altertümer von Pergamon, vol. 3, pt. 1. Berlin: Reimer, 1906, pl. 19.)

67 [118–119]
Samos, Heraion. View from point A, 1969. (Photo: A. Drymiotis.)

68 [120]
Samos, Heraion I, Geometric period. Plan.

69 [120]
Samos, Heraion II, Rhoikos period. Reconstruction. (Hans Walter, *Das griechische Heiligtum: Heraion von Samos*, Munich: Piper, 1965, fig. 58.)

70 [121]
Samos, Heraion II, Rhoikos period. Plan.

71 [121]
Samos, Heraion III, Classical period. Plan.

72 [122]
Samos, Heraion III, Classical period. Plan. (Hans Walter, *Das griechische Heiligtum: Heraion von Samos*, Munich: Piper, 1965, fig. 77.)

73 [122]
Samos, Heraion. Reconstruction of the great altar. (Hans Walter, *Das griechische Heiligtum: Heraion von Samos*, Munich: Piper, 1965, fig. 59.)

74 [123]
Samos, Heraion IV, Roman period. Plan.

75 [124]
Samos, Heraion. General plan showing four different periods. (Hans Walter, *Das griechische Heiligtum: Heraion von Samos*, Munich: Piper, 1965, fig. 86.)

76 [128–129]
Cos, Asclepeion. View from point F, 1969. (Photo: A. Drymiotis.)

77 [130]
Cos, Asclepion. Plan.

78 [131]
Cos, Asclepeion. General plan. (Rudolf Herzog, ed., *Kos: Ergebnisse der deutschen Ausgrabungen und Forschungen*, Berlin: Keller, 1932, vol. I, suppl.)

79 [132]
Cos, Asclepeion. Perspective of upper terrace from entrance A. (Rudolf Herzog, ed., *Kos: Ergebnisse der deutschen Ausgrabungen und Forschungen*, Berlin: Keller, 1932, vol. I, pl. 6.)

80 [132]
Cos, Asclepeion, Hellenistic period. Perspective from southwest. (Rudolf Herzog, ed., *Kos: Ergebnisse der deutschen Ausgrabungen und Forschungen*, Berlin: Keller, 1932, vol. I, pl. 40.)

81a [133]
Cos, Asclepeion. View of the site in relation to the sea, circa 1930. Rudolf Herzog, ed., *Kos: Ergebnisse der deutschen Ausgrabungen und Forschungen*, Berlin: Keller, 1932, vol. I, pl. 41.)

81b [134]
Cos, Asclepeion. View from upper terrace III looking north, 1969. (Photo: A. Drymiotis.)

82 [135]
Cos, Asclepeion. View from point I, 1969. (Photo: A. Drymiotis.)

83 [137]
Priene. General view from the west, circa 1898. (Theodor Wiegand and Hans Schrader, *Priene: Ergebnisse der Ausgrabungen und Untersuchungen in den Jahren 1895–98*, Berlin: Reimer, 1904, pl. 5.)

Comparative Plans
of the Sites Studied

3 Athens, Acropolis I, circa 530 B.C.
4 Athens, Acropolis II, circa 480 B.C.
5 Athens, Acropolis III, after 450 B.C.
Scale: 1:3400

8 Delphi, Terrace of Apollo, fifth century B.C.
Scale: 1:3400

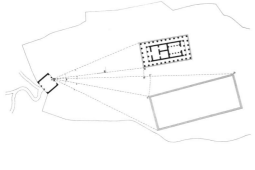

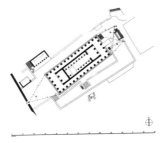

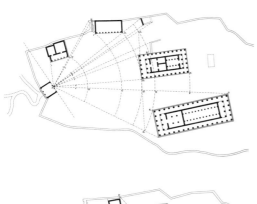

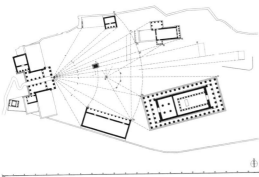

19   Aegina, Sacred Precinct of Aphaia, fifth
century B.C.
Scale: 1 : 1400

23   Miletus, Delphineion I, fifth and fourth
centuries B.C.
24   Miletus, Delphineion II, third and second
centuries B.C.
26   Miletus, Delphineion III, first century B.C. and
first century A.D.
27   Miletus, Delphineion IV, after first century A.D.
Scale: 1 : 1400

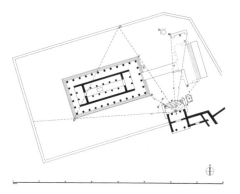

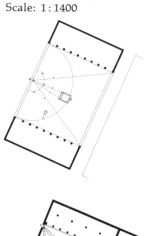

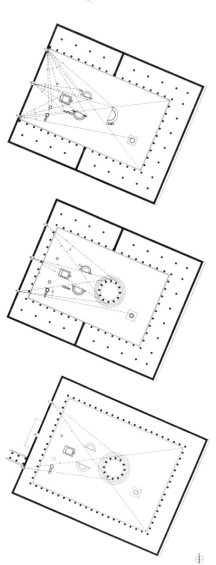

31 Miletus, Agora I, fifth and fourth centuries B.C.
32 Miletus, Agora II, second century B.C.
35 Miletus, Agora III, first century B.C. and first century A.D.
36 Miletus, Agora IV, second century A.D.
Scale: 1 : 5500

39 Olympia, Altis, Hellenistic period
Scale: 1:3400
49 Olympia, Altis, Roman period
Scale: 1:7300

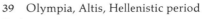

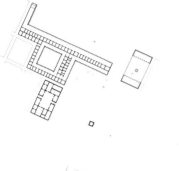

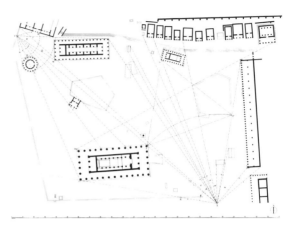

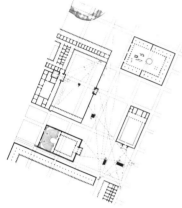

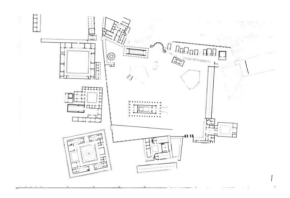

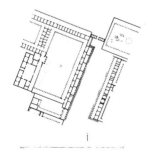

52 Sounion, Sacred Precinct of Poseidon, fifth
century B.C.
Scale: 1 : 1400

56 Pergamon, Agora, third or second century B.C.
61 Pergamon, Sacred Precinct of Athena, second
century B.C.
64 Pergamon, Altar of Zeus, second century B.C.
Scale: 1 : 3400

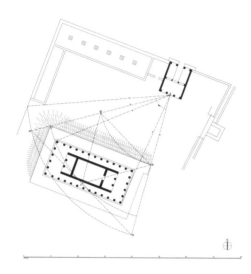

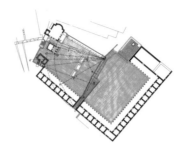

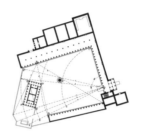

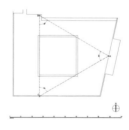

68 Samos, Heraion I, Geometric period
70 Samos, Heraion II, Rhoikos period
71 Samos, Heraion III, Classical period
Scale: 1:3400
74 Samos, Heraion IV, Roman period
Scale: 1:1400.

77 Cos, Asclepeion, second century A.D.
Scale: 1:3400.

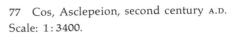

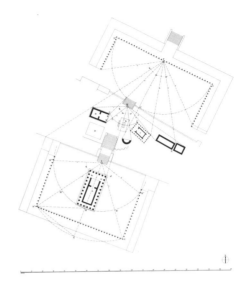

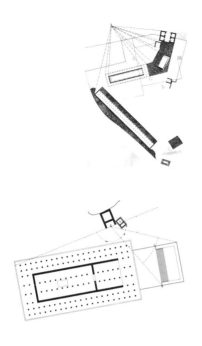

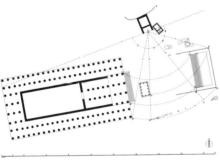

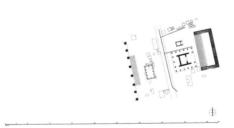

84 Priene, Agora and Sacred Precinct of the
Olympian Zeus, third century B.C.
Scale: 1:1400

96 Magnesia, Agora and Sacred Precinct of
Artemis, second century B.C.
Scale: 1:5500
106 Palmyra, Corinthian Temple, first century A.D.
Scale: 1:1400

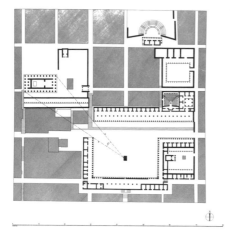

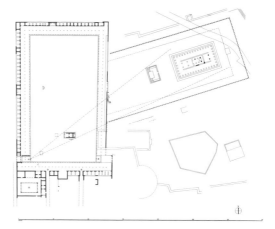

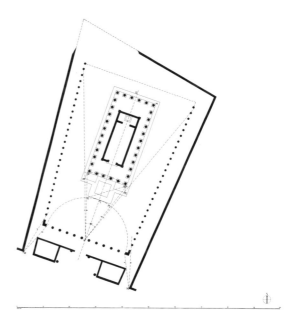

112   Selinus, Sacred Precinct of Demeter
Malophoros, sixth century B.C.
117   Sounion, Sacred Precinct of Athena, fifth
century B.C.
Scale: 1 : 1400

120   Priene, Sacred Precinct of Demeter, fourth
century B.C.
121   Priene, Sacred Precinct of the Egyptian Gods,
third century B.C.
Scale: 1 : 1400

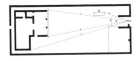

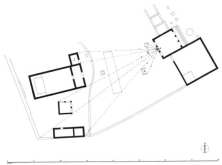

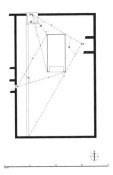

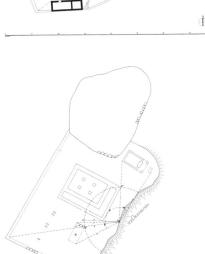

Athens, Acropolis. View from point A, 1968.

pages xxiv, xxv
Delphi, Terrace of Apollo. View from point C, 1968.

Delphi, Terrace of Apollo. View from point B, 1968.

Aegina, Sacred Precinct of Aphaia. View from
point A, 1968.

Miletus, Delphineion. View from the west, circa 1914.

pages xxviii, xxix (top left and right)
Olympia, Altis. View from point A, 1969.

page xxviii (lower left)
Olympia, Altis. View from point C, 1969.

page xxix (lower right)
Olympia, Altis. View from point B, 1969.

Sounion, Sacred Precinct of Poseidon. View from
point A, 1969.

Samos, Heraion.

page xxxii
Cos, Asclepeion. View from point I, 1969.

Cos, Asclepeion. View from point F, 1969.

page xxxiii
Priene, Agora. View from the east, circa 1898.

Magnesia, Sacred Precinct of Artemis. View of
site, 1936.

Palmyra. View showing arch and colonnade north
of Corinthian temple, circa 1917.

Sounion, Sacred Precinct of Athena. View from
point A, 1969.

Sounion. View of temple of Poseidon from the
precinct of Athena, 1969.

Architectural Space
in Ancient Greece

I The Discovery of the Ancient Greek System of Architectural Spacing

Man is the measure of all things,
of the existence of the things that are
and the nonexistence of the things that are not.

Protagoras,
quoted in Plato *Theaetetus* 152A

1 Investigation

The purpose of this study is to verify a theory concerning the ancient Greek system of site planning and to examine this system in relation to the culture as a whole rather than to check the precise details of its application at every site and at every period.

I investigated twenty-nine sites, two of which are Roman. The condition of these varies considerably, so that it is impossible to comment with equal assurance on all of them.* Only eight can be considered intact or authoritatively reconstructed: the Athens Acropolis III, the Asclepeion at Cos, the sequential layouts of the agora at Miletus, and the sanctuaries of Aphaia at Aegina, of Athena at Pergamon, of Zeus at Priene, of Demeter at Selinus, and of Poseidon at Sounion. These represent a very small proportion of the known sites, and certainly they do not suffice to demonstrate an irrefutable argument concerning the Greek system of planning. At some of the other twenty-one sites only parts of the layout could be observed and verified, so that my account of these is fragmentary. In short, the hypothesis presented here is based upon careful study of the few complete examples just mentioned and upon less thorough examination of a number of others. Imperfect evidence, I admit, makes it difficult to establish proof, yet in all the sites investigated—and they comprise the most important and best-preserved of those now known—I believe that I have traced the main outlines of a system of design. Even if future excavations show some of my conclusions to have been in error, I shall be content if I have succeeded in laying the foundation stone upon which others can later construct a valid and comprehensive theory. A preliminary hypothesis, whether it is right or wrong in detail, is essential to the process of scientific investigation: only after its initiation is there an incentive to test its accuracy.

* The author refers (here and throughout the book) to the condition of the sites as they existed in 1936. —Editor.

The most important discovery resulting from this study, in my view, is that the Greeks employed a uniform system in the disposition of buildings in space that was based on principles of human cognition. The few variations in the system are related primarily to mathematical formulae, which are described later in this chapter. Although most of the sites described in this study are sacred precincts, I am convinced that the system prevailing there represents a general theory of spatial organization—a theory of city planning.

As far as we can judge from excavations, the temples of ancient Greece were better built and the sacred precincts more carefully laid out than other parts of the city: this is why their remains are more numerous than those of secular buildings. The relationship between a sacred precinct and a secular layout was the same as that between a temple and a secular building: the first was a more perfect exemplar than the second. Just as we can consider a temple as representative of Greek architecture, so we may consider the layout of an entire sacred precinct as typical of all Greek spatial complexes. The layout of the agoras at Miletus, Magnesia, and Pergamon, for example (see Figs. 32, 96, and 56), appears to have been governed by the same laws as that of the sacred precincts. Only one difference was found between the sacred precincts and the secular sites, and this may be circumstantial, as there are so few well-documented examples of the latter. The difference is in the angles of vision and the distances between the buildings: in the secular sites it was not possible to determine whether a specific angle of vision was used. The reason for this was, certainly in part, that the poor condition of some of the sites did not permit a precise determination of the position of all buildings. But we can perhaps assume that it was also because, as has just been mentioned, less exact proportions and measurements were used in these sites than in the sacred precincts.

[3]

Differentiation between sites that were planned and those that developed over a period of time may appear to present another difficulty. I believe, however, that this study demonstrates that all changes obeyed the same basic rules of architectural spacing. It is true that the rules were not followed exactly on every occasion, but on the whole they persisted—and here lies the interest for us today. It is not always easy to remember that these complexes were built by the ancient Greeks not as isolated objects, as we see them today, but as parts of a dynamic urban environment. As elements of a city they were subject to contemporary conditions of growth and change. They were not designed to satisfy the aesthetic demands of modern man for an ideal layout, an ideal city, unrelated to an actual time or place.

If we have hitherto failed to recognize that the urban layouts of the archaic, classic, and Hellenistic periods were organized on the basis of a precisely calculated system, it is because we are strongly influenced, consciously or unconsciously, by the rectangular system of coordinates (in which every point is established by its position on a plane in relation to two lines intersecting at right angles). This system was completely unknown to the ancient Greeks. Their layouts were not designed on a drawing board; each was developed on a site in an existing landscape, which was not subject to the laws of axial coordinates.

When a man stands in a landscape and looks about him, he sees its various features as part of a system of which he is the center and in which all the points on the plane are determined by their distance from him. If he wishes to establish the position of a tree, for instance, he notes that it is to his left at a distance of about 7 paces and that a second tree is somewhat further to his left at a distance of about 14 paces, or double the distance of the first tree. He does not automatically establish the position of the two trees in relation to abstract axial coordi-

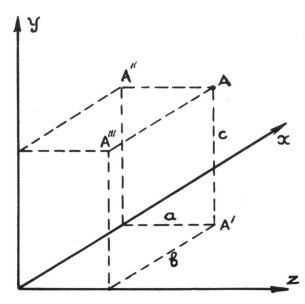

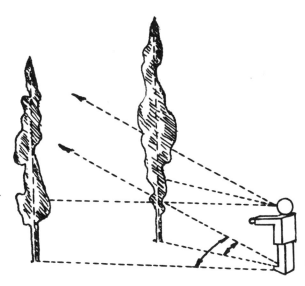

nates; he uses a natural system of coordinates. It was this system, known as the system of polar coordinates, that formed the basis of site planning in ancient Greece. The determining factor in the design was the human viewpoint. This point was established as the first and most important position from which the whole site could be observed: usually, it was the main entrance, which was often emphasized by a propylon. The following principles were used:

1

Radii from the vantage point determined the position of three corners of each important building, so that a three-quarter view of each was visible.

2

Generally, all important buildings could be seen in their entirety from the viewpoint, but if this was not possible, one building could be completely hidden by another; it was never partially concealed.

3

The radii that determined the corners of the important buildings formed certain specific angles from the viewpoint, equal in size on each site. These fell into two categories: angles of 30°, 60°, 90°, 120°, and 150°, corresponding to a division of the total field of 360° into twelve parts; and angles of 36°, 72°, 108°, and 144°, which resulted from division of the total field of vision into ten parts.

4

The position of the buildings was determined not only by the angle of vision but also by their distance from the viewpoint.

5

These distances were based on simple geometric ratios deriving from the angles of vision. Normally, the foot served as the basic unit of measurement, and the distances used were 100, 150, or 200 feet or those based on simple geometric proportions that could be determined on the site.

6

One angle, frequently in the center of the field of vision was left free of buildings and opened directly to the surrounding countryside. This represented the direction to be followed by the person approaching the site: it was the "sacred way."

7

This open angle was usually oriented toward east or west or in a specific direction associated with the local cult or tradition.

8

The buildings were often disposed so as to incorporate or accentuate features of the existing landscape and thus create a unified composition.

The viewpoint from which these measurements were taken was crucial and was obviously situated not just anywhere within the main entrance, or propylon, but at a specific place within it. The examples studied show that this point lay where the mathematical axis of the propylon intersects the line of its innermost step (i.e., the final step before one entered the sanctuary) at a height of approximately 5'7", the eye level of a man of average height.

A mathematical analysis of all the sites investigated is given in Tables 1–4, which show the development of the twelve- and ten-part system of architectural spacing. There is, on the whole, a conformity of mathematical relationships between certain angles of vision and certain distances between buildings. In some instances these relationships vary slightly. This does not necessarily imply that the system is faulty but rather that mathematical principles could not be precisely applied in every case. For example, some of the sites were developed over several centuries, and construction was carried out by different architects, who frequently had to change the original plans to meet new alterations or extensions. Sometimes the new composite plan could no longer follow the principles exactly because of new construction demands or because of a difficult terrain—factors that often upset calculations even today. Before pointing out inaccuracies in any given measurements, it is therefore necessary to take into account the far from ideal conditions under which most of the sites were constructed.

I believe that the physical limit of a structure (as seen from the vantage point) was measured from the edge of either the top step or the lowest step of the stylobate or from the edge of the cornice. All three measuring points were used, and this range of choice does not indicate a weakness in the system. In many cases the reason for the choice is apparent. For example, at the Athens Acropolis III (Fig. 5) the positions of the Erechtheion, the Parthenon, and the Chalkotheke were determined by their equidistance from point A. In the case of the Parthenon and the Erechtheion, this distance was measured to their lowest steps, because these are clearly visible from point A. But in the case of the Chalkotheke, the distance was measured to the top step (i.e., the base of the wall), as the lower steps are invisible from point A. The distance between the base of the wall of the Chalkotheke and the top step of the Parthenon is equal to the distance of each of these two buildings from point A.

It appears that one of the two following mathematical schemes was used (see Tables 1–4):

Twelve-Part System
The layout of the site was determined by angles of vision of 30°, 60°, etc., dividing the entire 360° into twelve equal parts. Distances between buildings were a, $a/2$, $a/2a$, or $a\sqrt{3}/2$; i.e., all were governed by a 60° angle. The area was thus divided into twelve equal parts.

Ten-Part System
The layout was determined by angles of vision of 18°, 36°, 72°, etc., dividing 360° into ten equal parts. In this case distances between buildings were a/b, $(a + b)/a$, $(2a + b)/(a + b)$, etc; i.e., they followed the golden section, which is determined by the isosceles triangle with an angle of 36° = 180°/5. The entire area was thus divided into ten equal parts.

There is but one complete exception: the precinct of the Egyptian gods at Priene, in which sight angles of 45° and 90° (i.e., an eighth part of 360°) were consistently employed. The reason may be that this was a foreign, not a purely Greek, cult.

It appears that all sites in the same city, or the same locality, employed the same mathematical system, for example,

Athens: Acropolis II and Acropolis III used the equilateral triangle (see Figs. 4, 5).

Cos: All three terraces used an angle of 360° (180/5) and the golden section (see Fig. 77).

Pergamon: The sanctuary of Athena, the agora, and the altar terrace used angles of 30° or 60° (see Figs. 61, 56, 64).

Priene: The agora and the sacred precincts of Zeus and Demeter used an angle of 36° and, in part, the golden section (see Figs. 84, 93, 120).

Samos: The Heraion of Rhoikos and subsequent layouts used 36° and the golden section (see Fig. 70).

[6]

Sounion: The sacred precincts of Poseidon and Athena used angles of 30° and 60° (see Figs. 52, 117).

There seemed at first to be several possible explanations for the use of two variations of the system: differences between cults and between individual deities; differences between the Greek peoples and in relations between cities; differences in architectural styles. Careful examination of the sites, however, eliminated two of these possibilities: differences between the deities had to be discounted, as both systems were used for the same deity (e.g., the sanctuary of Athena in Pergamon was based on the twelve-part system, but the ten-part system was used for her sanctuary at Priene); differences between the Greek peoples also had to be dropped, as both systems were in use in Ionian cities. The only plausible explanation seemed to be that the system depended on the architectural style employed. In general, when the buildings in the sacred precinct were in the Doric style, the twelve-part system was used; when in the Ionic style, the ten-part system was used.

In the following nine sites (listed chronologically) the buildings were in the Doric style and the twelve-part system was used:

Delphi, terrace of Apollo, sixth century B.C. (see Fig. 8)

Athens, Acropolis II, fifth century B.C. (see Fig. 4)

Aegina, sacred precinct of Aphaia, fifth century B.C. (see Fig. 19)

Miletus, Delphineion I, fifth and fourth centuries B.C. (see Fig. 23)

Olympia, Altis, fifth century B.C.

Sounion, sacred precinct of Poseidon, fifth century B.C. (see Fig. 52)

Miletus, Delphineion II, third century B.C. (see Fig. 24)

Pergamon, agora, third century B.C. (see Fig. 56)

Pergamon, sacred precinct of Athena, second century B.C. (see Fig. 61).

The following two sites with buildings in the Doric style used the ten-part system:

Cos, Asclepeion, fourth century B.C.-second century A.D. (see Fig. 77)

Priene, sacred precinct of Demeter, fourth century B.C. (see Fig. 120)

The following five sites with buildings in the Ionic style used the ten-part system:

Samos, Heraion II, in the time of Rhoikos, mid-sixth century B.C. (see Fig. 70)

Samos, Heraion III, of the classical period, late sixth century B.C. (see Fig. 71)

Priene, agora, late fourth century B.C. (see Fig. 84)

Priene, sacred precinct of Zeus, third century B.C. (see Fig. 93)

Magnesia, sacred precinct of Artemis, second century B.C. (see Fig. 95)

Sounion, sacred precinct of Athena, fifth century B.C., with buildings in the Ionic style, used the twelve-part system (see Fig. 117).

Athens, Acropolis III, fifth century B.C., with buildings in the Doric and Ionic styles, used both the twelve-part and ten-part systems (see Fig. 5).

The exceptions may perhaps be explained as follows:

Cos: The temple of Asclepios was built in the Doric style, but the angle of 36° and the golden section were used to determine the positions of the buildings and the distances between them. This may be because the sacred precinct was built toward the end of the Hellenistic period, when the architectural orders had become intermingled. The Doric columns here have Ionic proportions, and, indeed, the whole site already shows signs of Roman influence.

[7]

Priene: The sacred precinct of Demeter was also built in the Doric style but followed the ten-part system. This is the only outstanding exception to the rule. It could be argued that it provides evidence that the two systems were related to differences between the peoples of ancient Greece, although this is not borne out in other cases. As I have said, scarcity of examples prevents complete substantiation of my theory, and each case must be considered individually.

Sounion: The sacred precinct of Athena seems also to be an exception in that the building is Ionic, but the layout appears to follow the twelve-part system. As the location of the entrance has not been precisely determined, however, this example cannot be considered definitely contrary to the rule.

Athens: At the Acropolis III of Athens the majority of the buildings are in the Doric style, but the Erechtheion is purely Ionic. In general the 30° angle and proportions of 1:2 were used, but in subdivisions, angles of 18° and 36° were used with the golden section. It thus appears that both mathematical systems were used at this site, which contains important buildings in both styles.

Priene: The sacred precinct of the Egyptian gods, as has already been mentioned, was a foreign cult, and this may account for the organization of the site on the basis of 45° and 90° angles.

Selinus: The sacred precinct of Demeter appears to be organized on the basis of the angle of 90°, but the site is not sufficiently well documented for this to be certain.

There was yet another major difference between the two types of layouts in their organization of architectural space. In the first group, in which the Doric style and the twelve-part system were used, a path always formed an important feature in the disposition of the buildings in relation to the landscape. Sometimes this path divided the layout into two separate com-plexes; sometimes it acted as an open axis, left unobstructed as far as possible, so that the eye could look out far into the distance. By contrast, the layouts of the second group, in which the Ionic style and the ten-part system were employed, had closed views or presented an impression of enclosure, and a path was wholly incorporated within the layout. At the Heraion II (Rhoikos period) in Samos this effect of a closed view is particularly noticeable. After the destruction of the Rhoikos temple by fire, a large square was created in front of the new temple, Heraion III, but at the same time this was bordered by a long line of monuments that effectively closed the view (Fig. 71). In both the twelve- and ten-part systems it can be discerned that an attempt was made, whenever possible, to bring the outlines of the buildings into harmony with the lines of the landscape.

The open axis in the twelve-part system was sometimes oriented toward the east and sometimes toward the west. We can assume that this was consciously done so that a person entering the site by the propylon and following the open path had a clear view of the sunrise or sunset. In the case of the Athens Acropolis, for example, this axial view was held open in all of the three different layouts of the site, probably to allow an uninterrupted view of the sunrise at the time of the Panathenaic Festival. A similar intention can be observed in the closed Ionic layouts. As one enters the propylon at Samos, for instance, one faces a relatively low altar above which the sun can be seen rising from behind Mount Mykale.

Table 1
Use of the Twelve- and Ten-Part System

	Athens, Acropolis I	Athens, Acropolis II	Athens, Acropolis III
Date	ca. 530 B.C.	ca. 480 B.C.	after 450 B.C.
Angles of vision	3 equal angles of ca. 16°	$\frac{\pi}{6} + \frac{\pi}{6} + \frac{\pi}{6} + \frac{\pi}{6}$ $+ \frac{\pi}{6} + \frac{\pi}{6}$	$\frac{\pi}{6} + \frac{\pi}{6} + \frac{\pi}{6} + \frac{\pi}{6}$ $\frac{\pi}{10} + \left(\frac{\pi}{6} - \frac{\pi}{10}\right) + \cdots$
Distances	$x + 2 = 2y$ $y:2y =$ arithmetic progression	$x, \dfrac{x\sqrt{3}}{2}$ $\dfrac{x}{3}, \dfrac{2x}{3}, x, \dfrac{4x}{3}, \dfrac{5x}{3}$	$\dfrac{x}{2}, x, \dfrac{3x}{2}$ (golden section)
Measurements		$\dfrac{x}{3} = 30.8$ m $= 100$ pre-Periclean feet	
Proportions of buildings	Hecatompedon 1:2 Parthenon I $1:(1 + \sqrt{2})$	Hecatompedon 1:2 Parthenon II $1:\sqrt{8}:3$ Stoa $1:\sqrt{8}:3$	Parthenon $1:\sqrt{5}$ Chalkotheke $1:\sqrt{5}$ Erechtheion $1:2\sqrt{3}$ Propylaea $1:\sqrt{3}$
Basis of layout	Proportion 1:2 Clear view to east	Equilateral triangle Clear view to east	Equilateral triangle and golden section Clear view to east
General orientation of site	Eastward	Eastward	Eastward

Table 2
Use of the Twelve-Part System

	Delphi, Terrace of Apollo	Aegina, Sacred Precinct of Aphaia	Miletus, Delphineion I	Olympia, Altis
Date	530 B.C.	500–470 B.C.	479 B.C.	470–456 B.C. 4th cent. B.C.
Angles of vision	$\frac{\pi}{3}, \frac{\pi}{3}, \left(\frac{\pi}{4}\right)$	$\frac{\pi}{3} + \frac{\pi}{6} + \frac{\pi}{3}$	$\frac{\pi}{3} + \frac{\pi}{3} + \frac{\pi}{3}$	$\frac{\pi}{6} + \frac{\pi}{6} + \frac{\pi}{6} + \frac{\pi}{6}$ $\frac{\pi}{3} + \frac{\pi}{6}, \frac{\pi}{6} + \frac{\pi}{12}$
Distances		$2x : 3x$	$x : 2x$	$x : x\sqrt{3}$ $y : y\sqrt{3} : 2y$
Measurements			$2x = 30.8$ m $= 100$ pre-Periclean ft	$x = 80$ m $=$ approx. 250 Doric ft
Proportions of buildings		1:2 (lowest step)	Complete layout 2:3	Temple of Zeus 1: $\sqrt{5}$ Heraion ca. 1: $\sqrt{8}$:3 Metroon 1:2
Field of vision	Determined by the angle of 60°. Clear view to south.	Determined by equilateral triangle. Clear view to north.	Determined by equilateral triangle.	Determined by equilateral triangle.
General orientation of site	Southward	Northward		Northward

Sounion, Sacred Precinct of Poseidon	Miletus, Delphineion II	Pergamon, Agora	Pergamon, Sacred Precinct of Athena	Miletus, Delphineion III–IV
450 B.C.	334 B.C.	3rd or 2nd cent. B.C.	197–159 B.C.	Late Hellenistic to early Roman period
$\dfrac{\pi}{3}$	$\dfrac{\pi}{3} + \dfrac{\pi}{6}$	$\dfrac{\pi}{6} + \dfrac{\pi}{3}$	$\dfrac{\pi}{6} + \dfrac{\pi}{3} + \dfrac{\pi}{18}$	$\dfrac{\pi}{3} + \dfrac{\pi}{6} + \dfrac{\pi}{12}$
$x : x\sqrt{3}$	$x : 2x$	$x : \dfrac{x\sqrt{3}}{2}$	$x : \dfrac{x}{2} : \dfrac{x\sqrt{3}}{2}$	$x : 2x$
		$x = 52.40$ m $= 100$ ells		
Temple of Poseidon $1 : \sqrt{5}$	Complete layout $1 : \sqrt{3}$	Agora temple $1 : \sqrt{3} : 2$	Temple of Athena $1 : \sqrt{3} : 2$	
Determined by equilateral triangle.	Determined by equilateral triangle.	Determined by equilateral triangle.	Determined by equilateral triangle.	Determined by equilateral triangle.
Southward (Westward?)		Westward	Westward	

Table 3
Use of the Ten-Part System

	Samos, Heraion II	Samos, Heraion III	Priene, Agora	Cos, Asclepeion, Lower terrace
Date	ca. 550 B.C.	End of 6th cent. B.C.	2nd half of 4th cent. B.C.	300– 250 B.C.
Angles of vision	$\frac{\pi}{5} + \frac{\pi}{5} + \frac{3\pi}{5}$	$\frac{\pi}{5} + \frac{\pi}{5} + \frac{\pi}{6}$	$\frac{\pi}{10}$	$\frac{\pi}{5} + \frac{\pi}{5} + \frac{\pi}{5}$ $+ \frac{\pi}{5} + \frac{\pi}{5}$
Distances	$\frac{x}{y} = \frac{x+y}{x}$ (golden section)	$\frac{x}{y} = \frac{x+y}{x}$ (golden section)		$x : 2x$
Measurements	$x + y = 69.80$ m $= 200$ Ionian ft	$x + y = 69.80$ m $= 200$ Ionian ft		
Proportions of buildings	Rhoikos temple 1:2	Heraion 1:2		Lower terrace 1:2
Field of vision	Determined by triangle with angles of $\frac{\pi}{5}$ (36°)	Determined by triangle with angles of $\frac{\pi}{5}$ (36°)	Determined by triangle with angles of $\frac{\pi}{5}$ (36°)	Determined by triangle with angles of $\frac{\pi}{5}$ (36°)
General orientation of Site	Southward	Southward		

Priene, Sacred Precinct of Zeus	Magnesia, Sacred Precinct of Artemis	Cos, Asclepeion, Upper terrace	Cos, Asclepeion, Middle terrace	Palmyra, Small temple precinct
3rd cent. B.C.	158 B.C.	ca. 160 B.C.	2nd cent. A.D. and earlier	1st cent. A.D.
$\frac{\pi}{10} + \frac{\pi}{10}$	$\frac{\pi}{10} + \frac{\pi}{10} + \frac{\pi}{10}$	$\frac{\pi}{5} + \frac{\pi}{5} + \frac{\pi}{5}$ $+ \frac{\pi}{5}$	$\frac{\pi}{5} + \frac{\pi}{5} + \frac{\pi}{5}$ $+ \frac{\pi}{5} + \frac{\pi}{5}$	$\frac{\pi}{5}$
$\frac{x}{y} = \frac{x+y}{x}$ (golden section)	$\frac{x}{y} = \frac{x+y}{x}$ (golden section)	$\frac{x}{y} = \frac{x+y}{x}$ (golden section)	$\frac{x}{y} = \frac{x+y}{x}$ (golden section)	$\frac{x}{y} = \frac{x+y}{x}$ (golden section)
$x + y = 34.94$ m $= 100$ Ionian ft	$x + y = 104.8$ m $= 300$ Ionian ft	$x + y = 69.80$ m $= 200$ Ionian ft		
	Temple of Artemis $1 : \sqrt{3} : 2$	Temple of Asclepios $1 : 2$	Temple B $1 : \sqrt{3} : 2$ Altar $1 : \sqrt{2}$	Temple $1 : \sqrt{5}$
Determined by triangle with angles of $\frac{\pi}{5}$ (36°)	Determined by triangle with angles of $\frac{\pi}{5}$ (36°)	Determined by triangle with angles of $\frac{\pi}{5}$ (36°)	Determined by triangle with angles of $\frac{\pi}{5}$ (36°)	Determined by triangle with angles of $\frac{\pi}{5}$ (36°)

Westward

Table 4
Use of Exceptions to the System

	Selinus, Sanctuary of Demeter	Sounion, Sacred precinct of Athena	Priene, Sacred precinct of Demeter	Priene, Sanctuary of the Egyptian gods
Date	6th cent. B.C.	480–450 B.C.	2nd half of 4th cent. B.C.	3rd cent. B.C.
Angles of vision	$\frac{\pi}{2}$	$\frac{\pi}{6} + \frac{\pi}{3} + \left(\frac{\pi}{6}\right)$	$\frac{\pi}{10} + \frac{\pi}{5}$	$\frac{\pi}{2} + \frac{\pi}{4}, + \frac{\pi}{4}$
Distances		$x:2x$		$x : x\dfrac{\sqrt{3}}{2}$
Measurements				
Proportions of buildings		Temple of Athena earlier 3:4:5 later 3:4:5		Altar 1:2
Field of vision			Determined by triangle with angles of $\frac{\pi}{5}$ (36°)	
General orientation of site	Westward	Westward		

[14]

Unfortunately, there is not a single extant work on architecture—not even a sizable fragment—from ancient Greek times, although it is known that books on the subject were written by the best architects of every period. The only treatise on architecture that has been preserved from antiquity is the *De Architectura* of Vitruvius, the Roman architect and engineer. Although there are several passages in this work that might be cited in support of my hypothesis, they make no specific reference to the system of site planning I have just described, which, at the time when Vitruvius was in practice (about 46–30 B.C.), was no longer in use. Actually, Vitruvius makes no reference at all to methods of planning; he avoids the exposition of general theories and describes shapes and forms only insofar as they relate to building construction.

As writings on architecture were unavailable, I turned to other fields: to the philosophers Plato and Aristotle, the mathematicians Euclid and Proclus, the historian Plutarch, and the traveler Pausanias (although he gives only factual details concerning certain aspects of the sites he visited). Realizing the importance of relating the material achievements of an era to its ideas, I acquainted myself as thoroughly as possible with the literature of the period during which this system of group design prevailed. I paid special attention to philosophic and mathematical concepts that, in my view, seemed closely linked to theories of planning.

A Law Governing the Universe
In the first half of the sixth century B.C. Anaximander introduced into Greek philosophy the idea of a law governing all events in the universe. This idea inspired the legal concept of the polis, the Greek city-state of which every individual was unconditionally a subject.[1] Anaximander's own words on this, from the only fragment of his writings known to us, were recorded by Simplicius: "It is necessary that things should pass away into that from which they were born. For things must pay one another the penalty and compensation for their injustice according to the ordinance of time."[2]

Structure of the Universe
All Greek philosophers assumed that the center of the universe was a corpus; this was usually thought to be the earth, although sometimes, as in the case of the Pythagoreans, it was thought to be fire. We know that Anaximander, for example, held that the universe was a sphere with the earth as its center,[3] and the same concept was formulated by Aristotle: "Therefore all who hold that the world had a beginning say that the earth travelled to the middle."[4]

In connection with this theory most Greek philosophers believed that the universe was spherical, everlasting, and motionless.[5] This view was held by the Pythagoreans and Eleatics and also by Plato, who wrote "The earth lies in the center of a finite, though circular space."[6] The first thesis of Euclid's *Phaenomena* states that the earth lies in the center of the universe.[7]

The Finite or Infinite Nature of the Universe
Plato's allusion to a "finite" space touched on the most important issue in Greek philosophy: whether the universe was finite or infinite. According to Aristotle, "The first [problem] is whether there exists any infinite body, as most of the early philosophers believed, or whether that is an impossibility. This is a point whose settlement one way or the other makes no small difference, in fact, all the difference, to our in-

[15]

vestigation of the truth. It is this, one might say, which has been, and may be expected to be, the original of all the contradictions between those who make pronouncements in natural science."[8]

The Ionian philosophers maintained that the universe was infinite, and Anaximander, in particular, considered the infinite to be the basic principle of all things.[9] On the other hand, the Pythagoreans, the Eleatics, as well as the Attic philosophers—in short, all schools of philosophy except the Ionian—held that the universe was finite.

Aristotle offers several proofs of the finite nature of space: "Every sensible body has either weight or lightness. . . . Further, every sensible body is in some place, and of place there are six kinds [above and below, before and behind, right and left],[10] but these cannot exist in an infinite body. In general, if an infinite space is impossible, so is an infinite body."[11]

Until the late Hellenistic period Greek philosophy was influenced and sometimes dominated by a mathematical, or geometrical, concept of the universe. The earliest notion of a division of the universe is found in Homer, who divided it into five equal parts.[12] Later, the Pythagoreans asserted the ruling principle of numbers and believed in a geometrically ordered cosmos. The earliest Pythagorean, Petros of Chimera, taught that there were one hundred and eighty-three worlds "arranged in the form of a triangle, each side of the triangle having sixty worlds; of the three left over each is placed at an angle, and those that are next to one another are in contact and revolve gently as in a dance."[13] This theory formed the basis of the concept of the harmony of the spheres enunciated by Aristotle.[14] According to Proclus, the Pythagoreans always considered the equilateral triangle as the basic design of all created matter.[15]

The doctrine concerning the geometrical form of the universe appears also throughout the works of Plato and Aristotle and is reaffirmed later by Plutarch in his *Moralia*.[16] They maintained that the universe was based on five regular polyhedrons: earth was based on the cube, water on the pyramid, fire on the octahedron, air on the dodecahedron, and the heavens (light, or ether) on the icosahedron. Further, they held that these five polyhedrons corresponded to our five senses, resulting in the following relationships:

cube	earth	touch
pyramid	water	taste
octahedron	fire	smell
dodecahedron	air	hearing
icosahedron	light	sight

Euclid taught that the earth formed the mathematical center of the universe, and according to Proclus the universe was built up from the circle and the line.[17]

Geometrical Symbols in Religious Cults

The significance of mathematical symbols in religious rites led to the application of geometrical rules in the organization of space. Use of the symbols that I mention here can be traced for the most part to the Pythagoreans, particularly Philolaos, and in some instances to Plato.

Proclus calls to witness Plato, the Pythagorean authority, and Philolaos (in the *Bacchae*) concerning a theology based on geometrical concepts.[18] Proclus quotes Philolaos as saying that the Pythagoreans identified certain angles with specific gods: the 60° angle with Chronos, Hades, Ares, and Dionysos; the 90° angle with Rea, Demeter, Hera, and Hestia; the 150° angle with Zeus.[19]

Further, according to Archytas in his *Harmony*, the Pythagoreans taught that two stars forming an angle of 30°, 60°, 90°, 120°, 150°, or 180° exercised a powerful effect upon the earth and upon human well-being.[20]

According to Philolaos the Pythagoreans also identified certain geometric forms, such as the circle, triangle, and square, with specific gods, for example, Athena with the triangle, Hermes with the square.[21] A similar observation is found in Plutarch, who records that the Pythagoreans associated certain gods with certain numbers and signs, such as Athena with the equilateral triangle;[22] Hades, Dionysos, and Ares with 60° angle; Rhea, Demeter, Aphrodite, Hestia, and Hera with the 90° angle; and Zeus with the 150° angle.[23] Plutarch also states that the Egyptians identified the right-angled triangle having sides in the proportion 3:4:5 with Osiris and Isis.[24]

The relationships between angles and deities can be summarized as follows:

60° Hades, Ares, Dionysos, Athena, Chronos

90° Rhea, Hera, Demeter, Hestia, Aphrodite, Hermes

150° Zeus

Optics and Perspective

The mathematicians Euclid and Proclus both discuss optics. The contemporary laws of optical perspective given in the first definitions and theories in Euclid's *Optica* show that even at that time the rules governing the inclination of lines in space and the vanishing point of two parallel lines were formulated irrespective of whether they could be applied in an actual drawing. Proclus records that optics were derived from mathematics and were concerned with explaining the causes of false appearances, such as the meeting of two parallel lines in space.[25]

Numbers

Great importance was ascribed to numbers throughout antiquity. In illustration of this I quote from two sources:

Plato: "the great power of geometrical equality amongst both gods and men."[26]

Philolaos: "The nature of Number and Harmony admits of no Falsehood; for this is unrelated to them. Falsehood and Envy belong to the nature of the Non-Limited and the Unintelligent and the Irrational.

"Falsehood can in no way breathe on Number; for Falsehood is inimical and hostile to its nature, whereas Truth is related to and in close natural union with the race of Number."[27]

Certain numbers such as 10 and 12 had a particular significance for the Greeks. The great significance of 10 is referred to by almost all philosophers: Aristotle mentions it in his *Metaphysics,* and it was the subject of a special study by Philolaos in the second half of his book *On the Pythagorean Numbers.* "One must study the activities and the essence of Number" he wrote, "in accordance with the power existing in the Decad [*Ten-ness*]; for it [the Decad] is great, complete, all-achieving, and the origin of divine and human life and its Leader; it shares . . . the power also of the Decad. Without this, all things are unlimited, obscure and indiscernible."[28]

Proportion

The first representation of proportion found in classical writings is that implicit in the arithmetical expressions relating equal differences between two numbers, for example,

3 minus 2 = 2 minus 1

5 minus 3 = 3 minus 1.

Aristotle gives this example:

10 minus 6 = 6 minus 2.

This can be represented as

$a - b = b - c$ (sequential arithmetic progression)

$a - b = c - d$ (nonsequential arithmetic progression)

From the first we arrive at

$a + c = 2b$

and $b^2 - ac = (a - b)^2 = (b - c)^2$. (This proportion is used at Athens, Acropolis I; see pp. 29–30.)

Later, there is reference to geometric proportion. Archytas defined continuous geometric proportion as a sequence of constant ratios between two figures: the first is to the second as the second is to the third.[29]

$a:b = b:c$.

Discontinuous geometric proportion is

$a:b = c:d$.

Still later, harmonic proportion appears:

$(a - b):(b - c) = a:c$.

The first systematic theory of proportions is found in Euclid's *Elements* (Book V), although they were intrinsically known long before his time. To illustrate his theory Euclid used the regular pentagon and, by halving its basic angle, the golden section (although he did not use this name). He states, "A straight line is said to have been cut in extreme and mean ratio when, as the whole line is to the greater segment, so is the greater to the less."[30]

From this cursory review of classical sources

in philosophy and mathematics, it is clear that they contain several ideas that could give support to my hypothesis, although no specific mention is made of the system of organizing architectural space. The clearest allusion to such a system is found in these words of Philolaos: "And you may see the nature of Number and its power at work not only in supernatural and divine existences but also in all human activities and words everywhere, both throughout all technical production and also in music."[31]

The most likely reasons for the lack of contemporary reference to a system of organizing physical space are, as I have said, that no writings by architects have been preserved from ancient Greek times and that philosophers and mathematicians were less concerned with questions of physical design than with matters more directly related to their own pursuits. The lack of written records, however, does not alter my hypothesis concerning the system I have described.[32]

[1] Werner W. Jaeger, *Paideia: The Ideals of Greek Culture*, trans. Gilbert Highet, New York: Oxford University Press, 1945, p. 110.
[2] Ibid., p. 159.
[3] Ibid., p. 157.
[4] *On the Heavens* 2.13.295a13ff.
[5] Empedocles *On Nature*, in Hermann Diels, ed., *Die Fragmente der Vorsokratiker, Griechisch und Deutsch*, 5th ed., Berlin: Weidmann, 1934–1938, I, 31.324–325.
[6] Plato *Phaidon* 108CH.
[7] Euclides, *Opera Omnia*, ed. I. L. Heiberg and Henricus Menge, Leipzig: Teubner, 1883–1916, vol. 8, *Phaenomena et scripta musica*, ed. Henricus Menge (1916), pp. 10–12.
[8] *On the Heavens* 1.5.271b1ff.
[9] Jaeger, *Paideia*, p. 158.
[10] *Physics* 205b31.
[11] *Metaphysics* 11.10.
[12] Plutarch *Moralia* 5.13.390C.
[13] Plutarch *Moralia* 5.22.422B.
[14] *On the Heavens* 2.9.290b12ff.
[15] Proclus *Commentary on the first book of elements by Euclid*, Definitions XXIV–XXIX.
[16] *Moralia* 5.389.F11.
[17] Proclus *Commentary on Euclid*, Definitions XV, XVI.
[18] Proclus *Commentary on Euclid*, Prologue, pt. 1.
[19] Proclus *Commentary on Euclid*, Definition XXXIV.
[20] Archytas *Harmony*, in Diels, *Die Fragmente der Vorsokratiker*, I, 47.B2.436.6–8.
[21] In Diels, *Die Fragmente der Vorsokratiker*, I, 402.31.
[22] *Moralia* 5.381F.

[23] *Moralia* 5.363A.
[24] *Moralia* 5.379A.
[25] Proclus *Commentary on Euclid,* Prologue, pt. 1.
[26] "ἡ ἰσότης ἡ γεωμετρική καί ἐν Θεοῖς καί ἐν
ἀνθρώποις μέγα δύναται." *Gorgias* 508A.
[27] Philolaos *On the Pythagorean Numbers,* quoted by
Theo of Smyrna, 106.10, in Diels, *Die Fragmente der
Vorsokratiker,* I, 412.9–14. [English translation in
Kathleen Freeman, *Ancilla to The Pre-Socratic Philosophers,* Cambridge, Mass.: Harvard University Press,
1952, p. 75.]
[28] *On the Pythagorean Numbers,* in Diels, *Die Fragmente
der Vorsokratiker,* I. 411.8–13. [English translation in
Freeman, *Ancilla to The Pre-Socratic Philosophers,* p. 75.]
[29] Quoted in Porphyry *Harmonica of Ptolemy,* in Diels,
Die Fragmente der Vorsokratiker, I, 47B2.436.6–8.
[30] Euclid *Elements* (trans. Heath) 6.188, theorem 3.
[31] *On the Pythagorean Numbers,* quoted by Theo of
Smyrna 106.10, in Diels, *Die Fragmente der Vorsokratiker,* I, 412.4–8. [English translation in Freeman,
Ancilla to The Pre-Socratic Philosophers, p. 75.]
[32] For instance, it is undeniable that the Doric
metopes and triglyphs always had a ratio of 3:2, although this is not recorded in any book that has
come down to us.

3 Conclusion: Development of the Twelve- and Ten-Part System of Architectural Spacing

Origin of the System

A synthesis of my findings from examination of the excavated sites and of the classical literature makes possible the following conclusions.

Although my study was confined to examples of large open spaces for public use, I believe it can be safely inferred that the ancient Greek system of architectural spacing was universally employed, not only in the formation of urban spaces, whether on a large or small scale, but also in the disposition of statues and other decorative elements.

Aristotle contrasted the new Hippodamian system (νεώτερος καί ἱπποδάμειος τρόπος), or grid-iron plan, for organizing the layout of a city with the traditional system (ἀρχαιότερος τρόπος).[1] Prior to the use of the Hippodamian system (fifth century b.c.) all cities had been laid out in accordance with this traditional system, and they give the impression (as in Athens, for example) of having no comprehensive plan. But, when Aristotle contrasted the new system with the old, he was actually comparing two "systems," not a new system with previous haphazard growth. And it is possible to assume that the system of planning I describe here is that "traditional system" to which Aristotle referred.

The traditional system was devised to bring order into the disposition of buildings in a layout just as Greek philosophy brought order into the cosmos: the ordering of space on the earth would mirror the order of the universe.

As revealed in their writings, one of the most profound beliefs of the ancient Greeks was that man was "the measure of all things." This concept was given visible expression in the organization of the human environment: man himself was the center and point of reference in the formation of architectural space.

The ancient Greek writings also show the strong influence of mathematical laws on everyday life and thought. A mathematical image of the universe was taught by all philosophers. Proportion, or harmony, was considered of great importance and was used in every sphere. Thus, it might be expected that the buildings of ancient Greece would be disposed in space according to mathematical laws. The inherent logic of their siting was recognized by each succeeding generation, so that the harmonious development of the layout was ensured. The architects continued to follow the accepted theories of proportion, based at first on arithmetic and later on geometric principles. Certain practical considerations, however, such as the physical nature of the site and other technical exigencies, also affected the development and use of the system.[2]

Each site was divided into sectors, allowing for extensions within the over-all plan. The placing of the buildings was directly related to the contours of the landscape, because the Greeks continually sought to achieve order in space, no matter whether the space was natural or man-made. For example, when seen from the main entrance to the Altis at Olympia, at the southeast corner of the site, the outline of the Hill of Kronos, to the right, formed an essential balance with the temple of Zeus to the left (see Figure 40).

Since buildings were oriented according to

their relative position in space, the effects of optical perspective were important. (Parallel lines, for example, give the effect of diminishing space, open angles of magnifying it.) The effects of different shapings of space were studied (see Euclid's *Optica*), and the lines of buildings were brought into harmony with each other and with the landscape. The ancient Greeks wished to see for themselves the rising and setting of the sun; hence the sectors of the site leading east and west were usually kept open. It was man himself—not the god in the temple—who was the measure of all things.

As shown in the preceding chapters, there were certain differences between the Ionic and Doric sites. Although the small number of examples available for study makes it impossible to give definite reasons for these differences, a tentative explanation can be put forward, which is based on the contrasts between the Ionic and Doric views of the universe. The Ionians considered space to be infinite, and, since they feared endless space, they always enclosed the views in their layouts. The Ionians also favored the number 10, and it was fundamental in all their planning. It appears that they did not employ a different mathematical system for each god but used a single system based on the number 10. On the other hand, all other Greeks, both on the mainland and in the western colonial settlements, considered space to be finite and bounded. They had no fear of infinity, and their layouts always included a definite route that traversed the entire site and opened to the outside world. They divided space into twelve parts. According to the Pythagoreans, the universe was based on the equilateral triangle. Archytas refers in his *Harmony* to the dominance of angles of 30°, 60°, 90°, 120°, etc.[3] Although there are examples of numbers associated with the gods, there are too few to demonstrate positively whether certain mathematical systems were consistently associated with certain divinities.[4]

The development of the ancient Greek system of planning can be traced from the seventh to the first century B.C. It came into being with the birth of Greek architecture, reached the height of its development during the golden age of Greece, and fell into disuse when Greece declined. Its tradition was carried on in Hellenistic Asia Minor. A brief chronology of the development of the system follows.

Seventh Century B.C.
Concepts of the universe were still unclear. There were myths, but there was no philosophy; there was epic poetry, but no history. Site planning did not yet exist.

Sixth Century B.C.
Philosophy had its beginnings in Ionia, and there was interest in the laws governing the universe. In Miletus, Anaximander expounded his mathematical theory of the universe. The first observations were made of architectural space.

Ionic Order. The Heraion at Samos (Fig. 70), at the time of the second hecatompedon, represents possibly the first conscious attempt of the Greeks to organize space. About 550 B.C. the architects Rhoikos and Theodoros prepared the plan for the sacred precinct of Hera on the basis of the number 10, that is, dividing the space into ten parts.

Doric Order. The sacred precinct of Demeter at Selinus (Fig. 112) shows a full application of the twelve-part system of organizing space without use of the corresponding angles. Possibly the 90° angle was used.

530 B.C. Acropolis I at Athens (Fig. 3) represents the first known application of the twelve-part system on the Greek mainland. There is a balance of the major perceptible elements. Specific angular measurements were apparently not used. An arithmetical progression is observable along the length of the plan.

After 530 B.C. At the terrace of Apollo at Delphi (Fig. 8) the space was divided into twelve parts. The first observed use of the 60° angle was made here.

Ionic Order. End of sixth century B.C. In the reorganization of the Heraion at Samos the division of space into ten parts was continued from the earlier layout.

Fifth Century B.C.

Doric Order. Circa 480 B.C. At the Acropolis II at Athens (Fig. 4) and the sacred precinct of Aphaia at Aegina (Fig. 19) the same mathematical system was used: twelvefold division of the area; the equilateral triangle was employed, with its sides divided into three equal parts.

479 B.C. At Delphineion I at Miletus (Fig. 23) there was twelvefold division of the area; the equilateral triangle was used, with its sides divided into two equal parts.

470–430 B.C. At the Altis at Olympia the sacred precinct of Poseidon at Sounion (Fig. 52), and Acropolis III at Athens (Fig. 5) the same system was used: twelvefold division of the area; the equilateral triangle was employed, with its sides divided into two equal parts.

Fourth Century B.C.

Ionic Order. 350 B.C. The Asclepeion at Cos (Fig. 77), the sacred precincts of Demeter (Fig. 120), and the agora at Priene (Fig. 84) show a tenfold division.

Doric Order. 334 B.C. In the reorganization of the Delphineion at Miletus (Fig. 24) the twelvefold system was retained.

Third Century B.C.

Doric Order. The agora at Pergamon (Fig. 56) shows a twelvefold division.

Ionic Order. 300–250 B.C. In the reorganization of the Asclepeion (Asclepeion II) at Cos (Fig. 77) and of the sacred precinct of Zeus at Priene (Fig. 93) a tenfold division was used. The sacred precinct of the Egyptian gods at Priene (Fig. 121) shows an eightfold division.

Second Century B.C.

Doric Order. At the sacred precinct of Athena

at Pergamon (Fig. 61) a twelvefold division was employed.

Ionic Order. 160 B.C. The upper terrace of the Asclepeion at Cos (Fig. 77) and the sacred precinct of Artemis at Magnesia (Fig. 94) are the first two examples of an axial site plan.

Doric Order. The Altis at Olympia (Fig. 39) was reorganized to give more sense of enclosure.

Roman Period

Ionic Order. The axial layout of Palmyra (Fig. 106) clearly follows the Hellenistic tradition.

Aesthetic form was created by man to give pleasure to man. Pains were taken to place each structure and each group of structures to the utmost perfection so that they could be enjoyed from every viewpoint. Every detail was important: roof tiles, which would be seen by no one, had to be finished with the same care as the columns of a portico.

The ancient Greek system was total. It took all space into account, and all three-dimensional masses, man-made or natural, were incorporated as volumes in space. Voids as well as masses had their form, since together they constitute architectural space—the space that is created by man to enhance his sense of well-being.

Summary

It has been shown in Chapter 1 that the ancient Greek system comprehended certain basic tenets.

1
The relations between buildings had to be as simple as possible so that there would be the fewest possible lines in man's angle of vision. This principle extended to every detail.

2
Since gaps break the continuity and create a sequence of different elements rather than a coherent whole, care was taken to leave no optical gaps between buildings and to place them so that the line of one structure was directly con-

[22]

tinued by the next. For the same reason an effort was made to compose the outlines of the different buildings into a unified silhouette.

In every layout man was the focus of the creation. All sight lines started from man's position in space; all angles of vision were measured from the turning of his eyes; the length of his view decided the direction of the sacred way (looking toward the sunrise or out over the natural landscape); his height (that is, the level of his eyes) determined the line of horizontal perspective; his foot was the measuring rod for the length and breadth of all buildings. Space was created by man for man.

In Olympia, for example, the outline of the temple of Zeus is continued in one view by the Nike of Paeonios (Fig. 40), and in another view (Fig. 48) the line of the temple is continued to the left by the Hill of Kronos and the propylon and, to the right, by the Nike again.

3

The governing principle was that each form should be not only distinct but also visible in its entirety: from each viewpoint a building should either be seen as a whole or be excluded from the picture. No building could be obstructed so that it emerged only partially from behind another structure; nor could the continuation of a building be hidden from view. Adherence to this law was universal. One finds in every grouping that a building comes into view at the point where the view of another building ends. Precision and clarity were all-important elements in the formation of space. The sizes of the various buildings visible at any one time, as well as the spaces in which they stand, appear to man's eye in simple ratios such as $1:2$, $1:2:1$, $2:1:2$, $1:1:1$, $2:3:2:3$. Space is always partitioned harmoniously. The total mass of each structure was calculated and its effect determined. At times, as for example in the sacred precinct of Aphaia at Aegina (Fig. 19), these even appear to form a symmetry, which did not exist in reality.

The organization of every site was entirely rational and could be immediately comprehended from the entrance. The visitor's eyes were led to the most significant goal (usually an altar), which was approached by a clearly visible pathway, free of structures. But no organized routes led to the different buildings, nor was the site dominated by its largest structure. Every form was distinctly visible, and the visitor was at liberty to choose his own way. The entire layout was directly related to the landscape, and its design followed natural laws.

---

[1] *Politics* 7.10.4.
[2] [For information on construction methods in ancient Greece see Roland Martin, *Manuel de l'architecture grecque*, Paris: Picard, 1965, and Anastasios K. Orlandos, Τά ὑλικά δομῆς ἀρχαίων Ἑλλήνων, 2 vols., Athens: Library of the Archaeological Society, 1955–1960. The latter has been published in French under the title *Les matériaux de construction et la technique architecturale des anciens grecs*, trans. V. Hadjimichali, 2 vols., Paris: De Boccard, 1966.]
[3] Andreas Speiser, ed., *Klassische Stücke der Mathematik*, Leipzig: Orell Füssli, 1925, p. 9.
[4] [It is known that the most significant dimensions in the temples of ancient Greece always corresponded to round numbers of Greek feet. The author sought to determine whether this principle also applied in the Greek organization of exterior space. In taking measurements on the sites, the author used the following foot lengths:

Attic foot = 0.328 m
pre-Periclean foot = 0.308 m
Ionic foot = 0.349 m
Egyptian ell = 0.524 m.

Although the measurements of all important distances were checked according to these scales, the tables (pp. 9–14) record only the instances where the author was able to establish a definite correspondence with round numbers such as 100, 150, or 200 feet. In four cases the author was unable to examine the sites himself and was obliged to work from small plans that did not permit very detailed study.
There is still no complete accord on the size of the "foot" used in ancient Greece. The lengths used in this work differ somewhat from those given by W. B. Dinsmoor (in *The Architecture of Ancient Greece*, London: Batsford, 1950), the most widely accepted authority on the subject. Dinsmoor does not mention the existence of a pre-Periclean foot; he gives the Attic, or Doric, foot as varying from 0.326 m to 0.3272 m but states that "the Athenian foot was never quite so large as 0.328 m" (p. 195). He also gives the Ionic foot as 0.294 m, based on evidence from Didyma, "our most trustworthy source of in-

formation for the length of the Ionic foot" (p. 222). This is much smaller than the measurement accepted by Doxiadis. It is interesting to note, however, that 0.294 m was derived from "an axial spacing of 3.528 m" (p. 222), which is not far off ten times Doxiadis' unit of measurement (0.349 m). Dinsmoor also refers to the "Samian foot (so-called) of 13 7/8 inches," which is almost exactly 0.349 m. But Dinsmoor adds "this unit is very hypothetical" (p. 137). The question remains open, and several authorities (ranging from Hans Schleif to Stirling Dow) have been tempted to believe that the exact length of the foot was more or less arbitrarily determined on each site.]

II Description of Some Ancient Greek Sites

4 Use of the Twelve- and the Ten-Part System

The Acropolis at Athens, 530–437 B.C.

The Acropolis at Athens was inhabited for about three thousand years. Its various transformations during this long period, and particularly during its golden age, in the fifth century B.C., have been the subject of investigation since the beginning of archaeological studies. Unfortunately, the remains of individual buildings of the earlier periods are few and do not permit a complete reconstruction of the structural changes and developments of the site. Several theories, some partially conflicting, have already been put forward; I shall therefore not attempt to describe the development of the Acropolis in historical or philosophic terms but simply examine the organization of its architectural space.[1]

I have divided this development into three phases, beginning with the era of Pisistratus (560–527 B.C.) and his successors, when the general layout of the Acropolis is already recognizable, and passing over the earlier period, when the existence of only one building, the ancient temple of Athena,[2] is definitely known. During the first phase, 530–480 B.C., alterations were made to the ancient temple of Athena, a surrounding colonnade (pteron) was added, and the first stone Parthenon and the pre-Persian propylon were built.[3] In 506 B.C. a bronze quadriga was erected to celebrate a victory over the Boeotians and Chalcidians. There is no evidence, however, as to whether the Acropolis at this stage was consciously planned as a whole (Fig. 3).

During the period I have termed Acropolis II, 480–447 B.C., the pre-Parthenon, or Parthenon II, was built. Although there has been controversy as to whether this building was erected before or after the Persian invasion (480 B.C.), the prevalent opinion is that construction began in pre-Persian times and was never completed.[4] In addition to the Parthenon II, the Acropolis of this period consisted of the ancient temple of Athena, the adjacent sacred precinct of Pandrosos, remnants of the early propylon,[5] the southwestern building, and northern stoa. It

seems certain that the last two buildings date from this period. It is generally accepted that both were built after the Persian invasion, and they must have been built before the Periclean era, since they were removed at that time to make room for other structures.[6]

The plan of Acropolis II (Fig. 4) relates to the time before 447 B.C. when the building of Parthenon III began, heralding the new plan proposed by Pericles.

During the phase of Acropolis III, 447–437 B.C. the Acropolis was undoubtedly designed as a unity by Pericles and his advisers, even though it proceeded at first with gradual improvements[7] and due to political and religious circumstances was never fully completed.

The plan of Acropolis III (Fig. 5) shows the Parthenon, 447–432 B.C.; the Propylaea built by Mnesicles, ca. 435 B.C.; the Erechtheion, 421–407 B.C.; the Chalkotheke, completed before 400 B.C.; the colossal statue of Athena Promachos, 447–438 B.C. (C on the plan); the bronze quadriga, re-erected ca. 446 B.C. (K on the plan);[8] a square building northwest of the Erechtheion that covered the east part of the old north stoa.[9]

Acropolis I, 530–480 B.C.

Organization of the Site. The main entrance is through the early propylon.[10] Point A on the plan (Fig. 3) is at the center of the edge of the stylobate facing toward the ancient temple of Athena.

SIGHT LINES FROM POINT A

a to left corner of the ancient temple of Athena

b to right corner of the temple of Athena (B on the plan), passing the right corner of the quadriga (E on the plan)

c to left (northeast) corner of the Parthenon I (D on the plan)

d to the middle (northwest) corner of the Parthenon I (C on the plan)

e to the right (southwest) corner of the Parthenon I

ANGLES OF VISION FROM POINT A

Angles ab, bd, and de are all equal.

[29]

Angle $ae = 50°$.

DISTANCES FROM POINT A

Along the line AD we construct AB' equal to AB and AC' equal to AC.

We then find that $AD = AC' + C'D = AC + C'D$.

We also find by measurement that $AB = 80$ m and $AD = 160$ m.

Hence $AD = 2AB$.

If $AC' = x$, $AB = y$, $C'D = z$,

$x - y = y - z$ and $y:(x + z) = 1:2$.

This is an example of arithmetic progression.

We do not know the exact position of the relevant corners, nor can we be certain how much attention was paid to views of the distant landscape, since nothing remains of several buildings that are known to have existed[11] and that, with their accompanying monuments, may have been important elements of the layout. It can be asserted, however, that the field of vision between the ancient temple of Athena and the Parthenon I was then free of structures, for, to the extent that we can trust present evidence, it always seems to have been kept open. This view is directly oriented toward the east. The assumption that the space between lines b and c was always held free is supported by the situation of the quadriga, which was placed in position E on the plan: this position takes the line b into consideration and avoids blocking the field of vision between b and c.

Acropolis II, 480–447 B.C.

Organization of the Site. There is a single main entrance through the western propylon (Fig. 4). Point A remains in the same position as in Acropolis I.

SIGHT LINES FROM POINT A

a to left corner of the southwestern building.

b and b' to right corner of the southwestern building and left corner of the northern stoa. It is possible that b and b' are identical, since the exact position of the northeast corner of the northern stoa (H on the plan) is uncertain.

c to right corner of the northern stoa (D_1 on

plan) and left corner of the "northern wall."

d to right corner of this northern structure; d' to middle corner.

e to left corner of the enclosure sacred to Pandrosos.

f to the left (northwest) corner of the ancient temple of Athena.

g to the right (southwest) corner of the ancient temple of Athena (D_2 on the plan).

h to the left (northeast) corner of Parthenon II (G on the plan).

i to the right (southwest) corner of Parthenon II.

ANGLES OF VISION FROM POINT A

Angles bd, $dg = 30° = 180°/6$.

Angles ab, $fh = $ ca. $30°$.

Thus the plan is organized on the basis of an equilateral triangle AE_1E_4 with $AE_1 = AE_4 = E_1E_4 = 92.40$ m.

DISTANCES FROM POINT A

If arcs of a circle are described from point A to corners of the buildings, the following observations can be made.

The distance along line g to point D_2 at the corner of the ancient temple of Athena is equal to the distance along line c to point D_1 at the corner of the northern stoa;

i.e., $AD_2 = AD_1$.

Also, the distance to the middle (northwest) corner of the Parthenon (E_3 on the plan) is equal to the probable juncture of the Pandroseian precinct with the Hecatompedon (E_2 on the plan);

i.e., $AE_3 = AE_2$ (uncertain).

Further, a series of arcs touching one corner of each of the buildings cuts the line h at equal intervals;

i.e., $AB = BC = CE = EF = FG = 30.8$ m.

The distance AD does not appear in this series. It represents the height of the equilateral triangle AE_1E_4;

i.e., $AD = AE(\sqrt{3}/2) = 92.40 \times 0.866 = 80.02$ m.

Measurements show $AD = 80.0$ m.

[30]

The basic division of line h ($AB = 30.8$ m) is probably equal to 100 pre-Periclean feet (100×0.308 m). If this is accepted, all subsequent distances from point A are established at 100-ft intervals (100, 200, 300, 400, 500). Neither the size nor even the existence of the pre-Periclean foot as a unit of measure has been completely proved, however (see Chapter 3, note 4).

If $AE = x$, then $AD = 3x/2$ and $x/3 = 30.8$ m $= 100$ Attic feet.

Therefore the distances of B, C, E, F, G from point A can be expressed

$x/3$, $2x/3$, x, $4x/3$, $5x/3$.

FIELD OF VISION FROM POINT A

From point A, looking from left to right, the following views are possible:

the southwestern building within an angle of 30°

the northern stoa and the "northern wall" together within a second angle of 30°

a field of vision that is apparently open but is actually closed by the Lycabettos Hill, the sacred precinct of Pandrosos, and the ancient temple of Athena—all three within a third angle of 30°

a completely open field of vision together with Parthenon II within a fourth angle of 30°

The entire architectural scene is thus divided into four 30° sectors, and the central division, along line d, lies on the axis of the propylon. This means that the two remaining angles, left and right, between lines a and i and the face of the propylon, are also each 30°. In other words, the entire space is divided into six identical angles, each 30°, and this division, with the equilateral triangle that is derived from it, forms the organizing principle of the layout. The general view is enclosed on all sides except for a single open field of vision directly toward the east; the background of the other opening is entirely occupied by the Lycabettos Hill.

Acropolis III, 447–437 B.C.

Organization of the Site. The layout was prob-

ably determined either in 447 B.C., when Parthenon III was started, or in 437 B.C., when the new Propylaea was started. The plan was never fully carried out.

The main entrance is still through the Propylaea, and point A remains in the center of the front edge of the stylobate.

SIGHT LINES FROM POINT A

(* indicates that the exact position of these structures is uncertain.)

a to left corner of the steps beside the old north stoa on the northern slope of the Acropolis.

a' to nearest corner (southwest) of the house of the Arrephoroi.

b to right (southeast) corner of the same building.

c to left corner of the unbuilt, but probably planned, west porch of the Erechtheion* and left corner of the stylobate of the north porch of the Erechtheion.

c' to right corner of the west porch of the Erechtheion* (D_2 on the plan).

d to left side of the base of the statue of Athena Promachos (only the foundations remain, and I have assumed a conventional base). This line also leads to the right corner of the base of the porch of the caryatids of the Erechtheion (H on the plan) as well as to the right (southeast) corner of the stylobate and architrave of the east porch of the Erechtheion (E on the plan).

e to right corner of the base of the statue of Athena Promachos and left corner of the altar of Athena* (F on the plan).

f to right corner of the altar of Athena* and left corner of the altar of Zeus*.

g to left (northeast) corner of the lowest step of the Parthenon (G on the plan).

h to middle (northwest) corner of the lowest step of the Parthenon (D_3 on the plan).

k to left (northeast) corner of the wall of the Chalkotheke (D_4 on the plan) and right (southwest) corner of the lowest step of the Parthenon.

k' to middle (northwest) corner of the Chalkotheke (C' on the plan).

l to right (southwest) corner of the wall of the

[31]

Chalkotheke*. As the position of the southern wall of the Chalkotheke has not been precisely determined, its southwest corner cannot be located with certainty, but it was probably at the end of line l.

ANGLES OF VISION FROM POINT A

Angles ac, cg, gk, kl, all $= 30° = 180°/6$.

Thus an equilateral triangle AD_1D_4 is bounded by two symmetrical sectors of $30°$, with its axis on AG (line g).

The four equal angles ac, cg, gk, kl are divided into two parts (see Fig. 5), each of which has angles of $17°30'$ and $12°30'$ (approximately in the proportion $18°:12°$, or $3:2$).

Angle $ac = aa' + a'c = 17°30' + 12°30' = 30°$.
Angle $cg = cd + dg = 12°30' + 17°30' = 30°$.
Angle $gk = gh + hk = 12°30' + 17°30' = 30°$.
Angle $kl = kk' + k'l = 12°30' + 17°30' = 30°$.

But angle $c'h$ between the right corner of the west porch of the Erechtheion* and the nearest corner of the Parthenon $= 36° = 180°/5$. By dividing this important angle ($18°$ and $18°$) we arrive at line f', which may determine the right corner of the altar of Zeus*.

DISTANCES FROM POINT A

If an arc is described with center at A and radius AD_3 (the nearest corner of the Parthenon), it passes through the following points (from left to right):

D, the northeast corner of the house of the Arrephoroi (sensed but not visible from point A) $= 79.25$ m;

D_2, the southwest corner of the unbuilt western porch of the Erechtheum*;

D_3, the northwest corner of the lowest step of the Parthenon $= 79.25$ m;

D_4, the northeast corner of the wall of the Chalkotheke $= 79.70$ m; i.e., $AD = AD_2 = AD_3 = AD_4 = $ ca. 79.60 m.

If another arc is described with center at A and radius AC' (the nearest corner of the Chalkotheke), it passes through the center of the statue of Athena Promachos and is found to

measure 39.80 m; i.e., $AC = AC_1 = 39.80$ m. Hence $AC = AD/2$.

We also find that $DE = 39.80$ m.

Hence $AC = CD = DE = 39.80$ m; i.e., if $AD = x$, then $AC = x/2$ and $AE = 3x/2$.

If a line is drawn from point D_3 (the nearest corner of the Parthenon) parallel to the line AD_4 (the northeast corner of the Chalkotheke), it will cut AG (axis of the equilateral triangle) at point K.

Similarly, if a line is drawn from point H (southeast corner of the porch of the caryatids of the Erechtheion) parallel to AD_1 (the line c leading to the northwest corner of the north porch of the Erechtheion), it will also cut AG at point K.

Point K possesses similar remarkable relationships with other buildings (see Fig. 5).

FIELD OF VISION FROM POINT A

From point A, the field of vision from left to right comprises the following:

within the first angle of $30°$, the house of the Arrephoroi and an open view terminated by the Lycabettos Hill

within the next angle of $30°$, the Erechtheion, the statue of Athena Promachos, the altars of Athena* and Zeus* and a completely open field of vision

within the third angle of $30°$, the Parthenon

within the fourth angle of $30'$, the Chalkotheke*

The layout is thus organized within four $30°$ sectors.

Consequently, the location of the various buildings is determined by a division of the space into six or twelve parts, or by the angles and sides of an equilateral triangle derived from this division of space.

In certain instances, angles of $36°$ ($180°/5$), $18°$ ($180°/10$), and $12°$ ($180°/15$) seem to play an important role.

[32]

The field of vision from point A is enclosed on all sides except along the eastern axis (see Fig. 2). The buildings form two groups, the left group having an opening out into the landscape, which is closed in the distance by the Lycabettos Hill. This layout has many close similarities with that of Acropolis II. Most important, the open view to the east was retained in all three periods, although its relation to the entrance point A differed in each layout.

THE STRUCTURES

The proportions of the ground plans of the chief buildings were as follows:

Parthenon $\quad 1:\sqrt{5}$
Chalkotheke* $\quad 1:\sqrt{5}$
Erechtheion $\quad 1:2\sqrt{3}$
Propylaea $\quad 1:\sqrt{3}$
$\qquad$ (to the outer walls of the wings).

	South Side of Acropolis	North Side of Acropolis
		Mycenaean palace shrine
		1. Primitive temple of Athena (Doxiadis' "ancient temple of Athena")
ca. 570–566 B.C.	2. Hekatompedon (Doxiadis' "Parthenon I")	
529–520 B.C.		3. Pisistratid temple of Athena
488–480 B.C.	4. Older Parthenon (Doxiadis' "Parthenon II")	
480–479 B.C.	PERSIAN DESTRUCTION	
479 B.C.		5. Temporary shrine of Venerable image
447–432 B.C.	6. Parthenon (Doxiadis' "Parthenon III")	
439–437 B.C.		(Opisthodomos refinished)
421–405 B.C.		7. Erechteion
353 B.C.		(Opisthodomos demolished)]

[1] In addition to studying the literature on the Acropolis available in 1934 (Theodor Wiegand, *Die archaische Poros-Architektur der Acropolis zu Âthen*, Leipzig, 1904; Wilhelm Dörpfeld, "Das Hekatompedon in Athen," Deutsches Archäologisches Institut, *Jahrbuch* 34, 1919, pp. 1–40; Gerhard Rodenwaldt, *Die Akropolis*, Berlin: Deutscher Kunstverlag, 1930; Walter Judeich, *Topographie von Athen*, 2nd ed., Munich: Beck, 1931), I made careful investigations and took measurements on the site. Comparison of my own conclusions with the published plans convinced me that the latter were inadequate for my needs, since, no matter how carefully they had been drawn, they had been made for different purposes. I therefore present my own drawings here, based on the most precise measurements I was able to make. It is my opinion, however, that angles and distances cannot be determined exactly until a complete trigonometric survey has been made of the Acropolis. (This is true also of all the other sites I have examined.)
[2] [In the original text (*Raumordnung im griechischen Städtebau*) Doxiadis referred to the ancient temple of Athena (i.e., the pre-Pisistratid temple) as the Hecatompedon. According to more recent studies, however, this name was given to the structure that he has called Parthenon I, on the site of the present Parthenon. See William B. Dinsmoor, "The Hekatompedon on the Athenian Acropolis," *American Journal of Archaeology* 51, 1947, p. 140.]
[3] See Judeich, *Topographie von Athen*, p. 66.
[4] [The dates now generally accepted are given in the following table based on Dinsmoor, "The Hekatompedon," p. 140:

[5] [According to Dinsmoor, the ancient propylon, "being a secular building . . . was repaired after the departure of the Persians" (*The Architecture of Ancient Greece*, London, 1959, p. 198).]
[6] Judeich, *Topographie von Athen*, p. 246. [Studies made since that of Judeich have cast doubts on the early existence of the northern stoa, but the existence and position of the southwestern building are still generally accepted. Gorham P. Stevens considers the latter to have been "a dwelling for priests or priestesses, or an office of some kind"; in his view, "the building was still standing when Mnesicles started the Propylaea in 437 B.C." (*The Periclean Entrance Court of the Acropolis of Athens*, Cambridge, Mass.: Harvard University Press, 1936, pp. 69–70). Architectural fragments and roof elements of other buildings have been found, but their position is unknown.]
[7] Judeich, *Topographie von Athen*, p. 79.
[8] *Ibid.*, p. 239.
[9] [Doxiadis does not mention the boundary wall of the sanctuary of the Brauronian Artemis, built in the fifth century B.C. between the Propylaea and the Chalkotheke, nor the Mycenaean retaining wall of the terrace of the old temple of Athena, behind the great statue of Athena Promachos. Both are included in Doxiadis' drawing (Fig. 2) but not in his plan (Fig. 5). The height of these walls has not been definitely established. The drawing shows them as low boundary walls. According to Gorham P. Stevens, however, the sanctuary of the Brauronian Artemis was bounded by a high wall "bordered on the east and south with stoa-like structures," and the east stoa "must have concealed a large part of the Parthenon from those emerging from the east portico of the Propylaea" (*The Periclean Entrance Court of the Acropolis,*

p. 18). This statement should perhaps be related to Stevens' introductory remarks in the same work (p. 1) concerning the layout of pre-Hellenistic sites: "The trained architect admires the beauty of the individual buildings of early date, but he calls the grouping of the buildings by its real name—a mess. And he wonders how the ancient Greeks, who were famous for their keen artistic appreciations of all kinds, tolerated such unsightly group planning." Stevens' ground plan of the sanctuary of the Brauronian Artemis has been reproduced in almost all subsequent plans of the Acropolis, but agreement has not been reached on the "stoa-like structure" along its eastern boundary or the height of its surrounding walls. In the same study (p. 60) Stevens gives his reasons for assuming that the Mycenaean wall behind the statue of Athena Promachos was 4–5 meters high, but this also remains to be proved.]
[10] The propylon is drawn according to the reconstruction of Dörpfeld ("Das Hekatompedon," pl. 1) and Judeich (*Topographie von Athen*, fig. 23).
[11] Wiegand, *Die archaische Poros-Architektur der Acropolis*, p. 148.

Works Consulted by the Author
Dörpfeld, Wilhelm. "Das Hekatompedon in Athen." Deutsches Archäologisches Institut. *Jahrbuch* 34, 1919.

Judeich, Walter. *Topographie von Athen.* 2nd ed. Munich: Beck, 1931.

Rodenwaldt, Gerhard. *Die Akropolis.* Berlin: Deutscher Kunstverlag, 1930.

Wiegand, Theodor. *Die archaische Poros-Architektur der Acropolis zu Athen.* Leipzig: Fisher, 1904.

Additional References
Bundgaard, Jens A. *Mnesicles: A Greek Architect at Work.* Copenhagen: Gyldendal, 1957.

Dinsmoor, William B. "The Burning of the Opisthodomos at Athens." *American Journal of Archaeology* 36, 1932, pp. 143–172, 307–326.

———. "The Hekatompedon on the Athenian Acropolis." *AJA* 51, 1947.

Dörpfeld, Wilhelm, and Schleif, Hans. *Erechtheion.* Berlin: Mittler, 1942.

Raubitschek, Antony E. *Dedications from the Athenian Akropolis.* Cambridge, Mass.: Archaeological Institute of America, 1949.

Stevens, Gorham P. "Architectural Studies Concerning the Acropolis of Athens." *Hesperia* 15, 1946, pp. 75–106.

———. *The Erechtheum.* Edited by James M. Paton. Cambridge, Mass.: Harvard University Press, 1927.

———. *The Periclean Entrance Court of the Acropolis of Athens.* Cambridge, Mass.: Harvard University Press, 1936.

———. "The Setting of the Periclean Parthenon." *Hesperia,* suppl. 3, 1940.

1 Athens, Acropolis. View from point A, 1968.

2 Athens, Acropolis III, after 450 B.C. Perspective from point A.

3 Athens, Acropolis I, circa 530 B.C. Plan.

4 Athens, Acropolis II, circa 480 B.C. Plan.

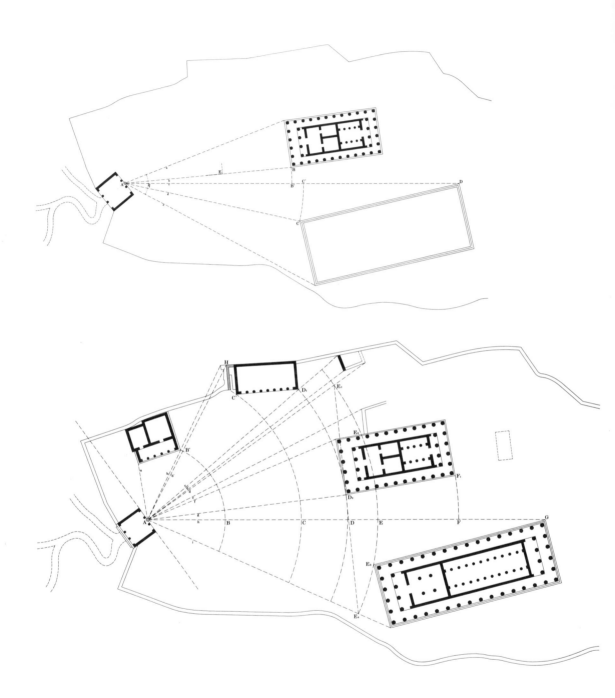

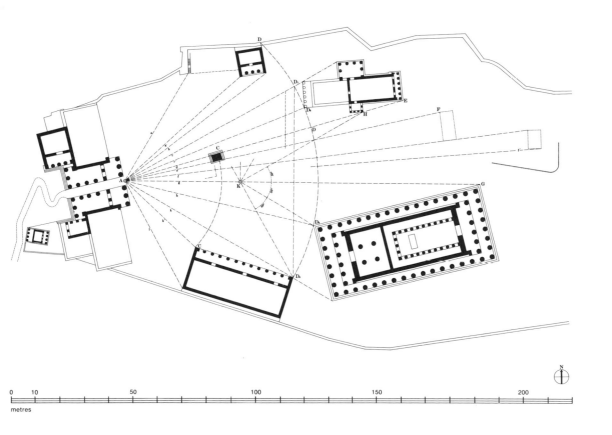

0   10   50   100   150   200

metres

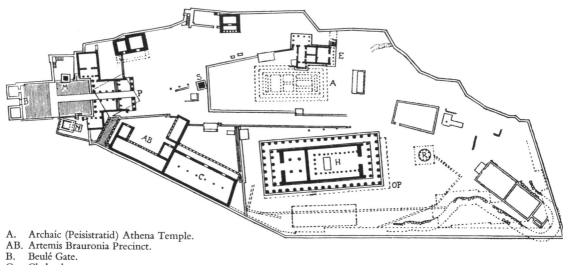

A.   Archaic (Peisistratid) Athena Temple.
AB. Artemis Brauronia Precinct.
B.   Beulé Gate.
C.   Chalcotheca.
E.   Erechtheum.
H.   Hecatompedos Naos (Parthenon)
M.   Monument of Agrippa.
N.   Nike Temple.
OP. Older Parthenon.
P.   Propylaea.
R.   Roma and Augustus Temple.
S.   Statue of Athena Promachos.

5 Use of the Twelve-Part System

The Temple Terrace of Apollo at Delphi, Fifth Century B.C.

Excavations of the sacred precinct of Delphi are still incomplete, and the published reports on them do not present a clear picture of the entire site; there are even differences of opinion concerning the structures that have been fully excavated. I have therefore ventured to draw only one general conclusion regarding the site as a whole, which is supported by the plans that have so far been published. (Rechecking of measurements on the spot would be a tremendously difficult and elaborate operation, as the site is on a steep mountain side.) A visual contrast between the two largest building masses, the temple of Apollo and the theater, was prevented. From both the main entrance to the site and from the southeast entrance, the theater was completely hidden by the temple; and from other entrances, views of it were blocked by retaining walls and similar structures (see Fig. 14).

The temple terrace is undoubtedly the most important feature of the site, but my studies of it are merely preliminary. Scholars have established that it passed through two great building phases. The first layout included the temple said to have been built by the architects Trophonios and Agamedes,[1] probably in the first half of the sixth century B.C. (unfortunately there are too few traces of this building to permit examination), and the second comprised the great temple built with the aid of the Alkmaeonid family about 530 B.C.[2] The exact points of access to this temple terrace are uncertain, but it seems likely that the first general view of the temple from the sacred way was obtained from point A (Fig. 8), just south of the great altar erected by the Greeks of Chios, even though it is possible that there was no direct access to the temple from this point. The second view was from point B, the only entrance of which we are positive (this was not framed by a gateway). At this point the sacred way turned to enter the temple terrace itself. A door in the western wall of the precinct may have served as

a third entrance to the other end of the temple. The great altar was dedicated in 476 B.C.

Several monuments were added in the Hellenistic period, including the double columns (D on the plan);[3] a statue of Eumenes II, King of Pergamon, 182 B.C. (E on the plan; and see Fig. 11); a statue of Aemilius Paullus, 168 B.C. (F on the plan; and see Fig. 12).

Organization of the Site. The precinct developed gradually over the years. The great temple of Apollo was built about 530 B.C.

SIGHT LINES FROM POINT A

Point A lies in the center of the opening just south of the great altar.

a to left (northeast) corner of the temple.

b to left corner of the great altar, right (northwest) corner of temple.

Angle $ab = 60° = 180°/3$.

SIGHT LINES FROM POINT B

Point B, though more important, can be located with less certainty, as it cannot be placed centrally in a clearly marked entrance.

c to right corner of great altar, left (northeast) corner of the temple

d to right corner of the temple

Angle $cd = 60° = 180°/3$.

The accuracy of lines c and d is confirmed by the placing of the later Hellenistic monuments D, E, and F, which shows regard for these lines. In fact lines c and d explain the positions of D and F, which (unaccountably, as it may seem to us) bear no relation to the axis of the temple. The sight lines may also account for the position of the column south of the temple terrace.[4] All these monuments were placed so that they would form a symmetrical composition with the façade of the temple when seen from one or other of the main viewpoints; no account was taken of their position in relation to the geometrical axis of the temple.

SIGHT LINES FROM POINT C

The position of point C is somewhat uncertain: it lies on the direct axis of the temple and forms an isosceles triangle with the corners of the west façade, whose angles measure $180°/4$, $3 \times 180°/8$, $3 \times 180°/8$.

---

[1] See Homeric Hymn, "To Apollo," lines 294–299.
[2] [Dinsmoor states that the second stone temple of Apollo was undertaken in the last quarter of the sixth century "to replace the structure burnt in 548 B.C. . . . The plan was almost identical with that of the later temple which took its place after the destructive earthquake of 373 B.C." (*The Architecture of Ancient Greece*, London: Batsford, 1950, pp. 91–92).]
[3] [While Doxiadis was preparing this dissertation in Berlin (originally published as *Raumordnung im griechischen Städtebau*, Heidelberg, 1937), Pierre de la Coste-Messelière was completing a thesis in Paris that was published in 1936 under the title *Au Musée de Delphes*. In his study La Coste-Messelière revised several of the previous positions of votive monuments, including the column of Aemilius Paullus and the double columns of Lycos Diocles, which Doxiadis had placed according to the opinion of Pomtow (see A. F. von Pauly, ed., *Real-Encyclopädie der classischen Altertumswissenschaft*, suppl. 4, 1924, map on p. 1199). The site of the column of Aemilius Paullus has been established in the corner of the lower terrace, slightly east of the position accepted by Doxiadis (see Fig. 16, reproduced from Pierre de la Coste-Messelière, *Delphes*, Paris, 1943). Even with the statue in this changed position, Doxiadis' theory still seems to hold, except that his line *c* from point *B* now touches the northwest corner of the column of Aemilius Paullus instead of the southeast corner, and line *a* from point *A* touches the southeast corner. The exact position of the double columns of Lycos Diocles—dedicated by the ladies of the family of Lycos and Diocles, "sans doute deux Delphiens" (Emile Bourguet, *Les Ruines de Delphes*, Paris, 1914, pp. 148–149)—is still in some doubt. The position assigned to them beside the temple of Apollo by Pomtow is not now considered correct: Pierre Amandry believes that this was probably the site of the column of Nicopolis ("Chronique des fouilles en 1947," *Bulletin de correspondance hellénique* 71–72, 1947–1948, p. 451). La Coste-Messelière showed the Lycos Diocles columns south of the open area below the Athenian portico (*Au Musée de Delphes*, no. 21 on plan), but this position is still not definitely established (Amandry, "Chronique des fouilles de 1943 à 1945," *Bulletin de correspondance hellénique* 68–69, 1944–1945, p. 439)].
[4] [In the original edition of this work (*Raumordnung im griechischen Städtebau*, p. 39), Doxiadis referred to this column as the Nike column of Paeonios. This attribution was based on the statements of Fernand Courby (*La Terrasse du temple*, pt. 1, p. 302) and Pomtow ("Delphoi," pt. 1, pp. 1308–1310). The triangular-shaped column at Delphi bore such similarity to the Nike column at Olympia that Pomtow was convinced that the Delphi column, the Nike of the Messenians, was surmounted by the original Nike statue in gilded bronze by Paeonios and that the marble statue in Olympia was a later copy. Pausanias

does not mention this monument. According to Georges Daux, "As to the Victory of the Messenians, it is possible that the statue had been pillaged from the triangular column prior to this period" (*Pausanias à Delphes*, Paris, 1936, p. 163). Daux's later opinion was that there were probably two triangular columns ("Inscriptions et monuments archaiques de Delphes," *Bulletin de correspondance hellénique* 61, 1937, p. 72) and that both stood on the lower terrace, south of the temple of Apollo. The exact position of these is still uncertain, however (see La Coste-Messelière, *Delphes*, no. 25 on plan, reproduced here as Fig. 16). They are now known as the Columns of the Messenians.]

Works Consulted by the Author
Bourguet, Emile. *Les Ruines de Delphes*. Paris: Fontemoing, 1914.

Courby, Fernand. *La Terrasse du temple*, pt. 1. Fouilles de Delphes, vol. 2. Paris: De Boccard, 1927.

Pomtow, H. "Delphoi," pt. 1. In A. F. von Pauly, ed., *Real-Encyclopädie der classischen Altertumswissenschaft*, suppl. 4, Stuttgart: Metzler, 1924, pp. 1189–1432.

———. "Die Paionios-Nike in Delphi." *Deutsches Archäologisches Institut Jahrbuch* 37, 1922.

Schober, Friedrich. "Delphoi," pt. 2. In A. F. von Pauly, ed., *Real-Encyclopädie der classischen Altertumswissenschaft*, suppl. 5, 1931, pp. 59–152.

Tournaire, Albert. *Relevés et restaurations*, pt. 1. Fouilles de Delphes, vol. 2. Paris: Fontemoing, 1902.

Additional References
Amandry, Pierre. "Chronique des fouilles de 1943 à 1945," *Bulletin de correspondance hellénique* 68–69, 1944–1945, pp. 439–441.

———. "Chronique des fouilles en 1947," *BCH* 71–72, 1947–1948, pp. 445–452.

———. "Recherches à Delphes, 1938–1953," International Congress of Classical Studies, 2nd, 1954, *Acta Congressus Madvigiani*, Copenhagen: Munksgaard, 1957–1958, I, pp. 325–340.

Daux, Georges. *Inscriptions*, pt. 3, 2. Fouilles de Delphes, vol. 3, Paris, 1943.

———. "Inscriptions et monuments archaiques de Delphes," *BCH* 61, 1937, pp. 67–72.

———. *Pausanias à Delphes*. Paris: Picard, 1936.

Kähler, Heinz. *Der Fries vom Reiterdenkmal des Aemilius Paullus in Delphi*. Berlin: Mann, 1965.

La Coste-Messelière, Pierre de, *Au Musée de Delphes*. Paris: De Boccard, 1936.

———. *Delphes*. Paris: Editions du Chêne, 1943.

7 Delphi, Terrace of Apollo. View from point C, 1968.

8 Delphi, Terrace of Apollo. Plan of temple.

9 Delphi, Terrace of Apollo. Elevation of temple
and terrace. (Courby.)

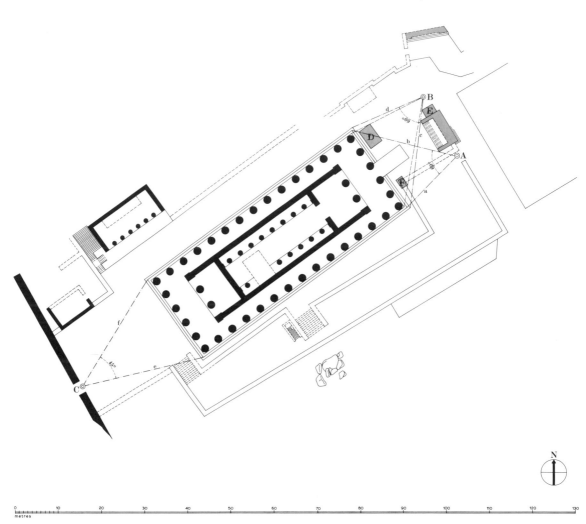

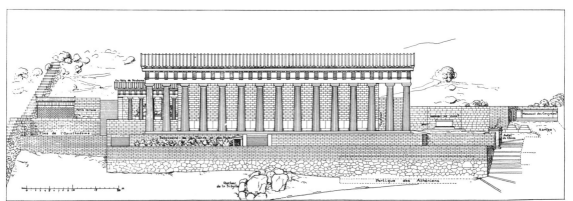

10   Delphi, Terrace of Apollo. View from point B,
1968.

11   Delphi, Terrace of Apollo. Monument to
Eumenes II. (Courby.)

12   Delphi, Terrace of Apollo. Monument to
Aemilius Paullus. (Kähler.)

13   Delphi, Terrace of Apollo. Restoration.
(Tournaire.)

14   Delphi, Terrace of Apollo. Sketch showing view
from the southwest in ancient times.

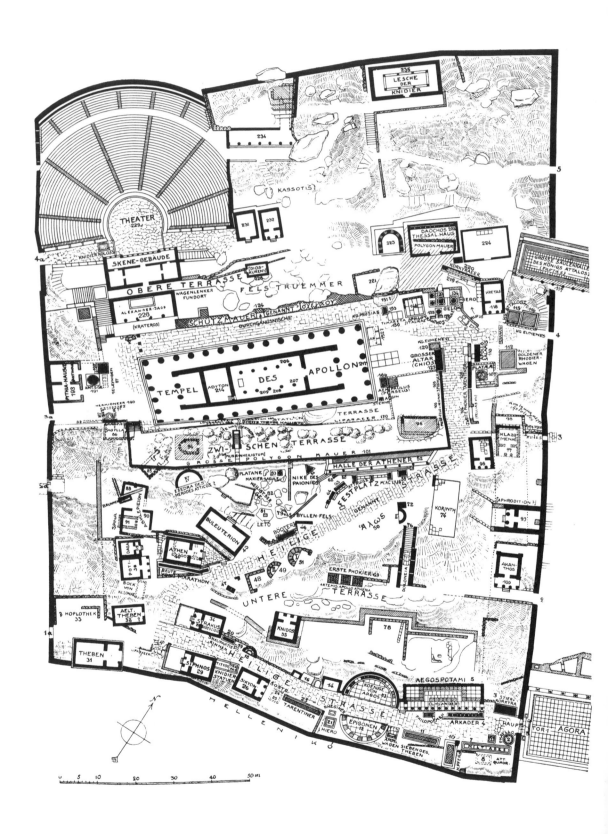

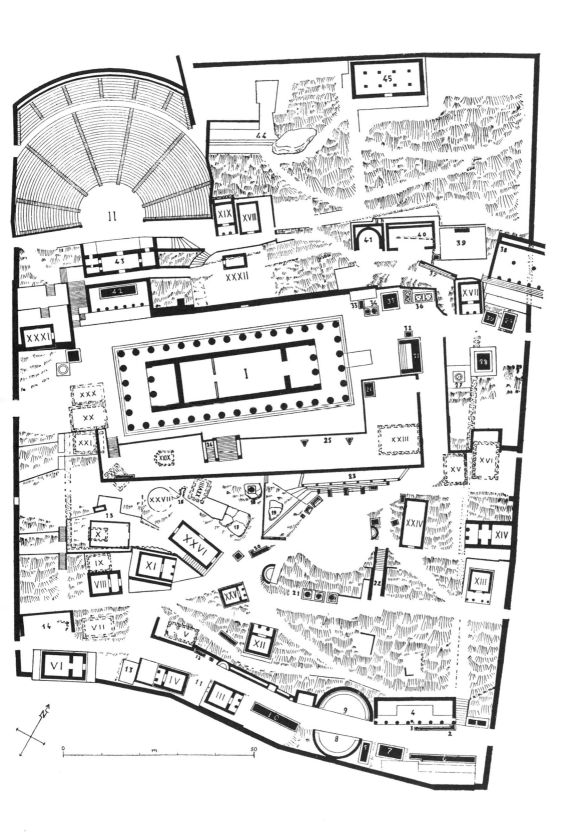

The Sacred Precinct of Aphaia at Aegina, Fifth Century B.C.

The remains of buildings in the sacred precinct of Aphaia (Fig. 18) show that there were three major periods of construction, but only for the last period is it possible to reconstruct an accurate plan (Fig. 19), as traces of the layout during the two earlier periods—especially indications of the position of the temples—are insufficient.[1] The final temple of Aphaia and its contemporary precinct were "built roughly between 500 and 470 B.C., and were probably started nearer to the earlier than the later date."[2] The structures erected at the same time as the temple—they can be recognized, as they follow the same orientation—all form part of a single cohesive plan. They comprise the large altar (Fig. 21), the propylon, three of the terrace walls, and three bases for monuments on the east part of the terrace.[3] These three monument bases are shown as S, M, and N in Figure 19. The only monument of an earlier period that might possibly have remained in its original position is an ancient Ionic votive column,[4] the site of which is shown as E in Figure 19.

Organization of the Site. The precinct was laid out between 500 and 470 B.C. Entry was through the propylon, and point A, center of the inner edge of the propylon floor, represents the geometric center of the complex.

SIGHT LINES FROM POINT A

(* indicates that the exact position of this structure is uncertain.)

a to left (southwest) corner of temple (D'' on the plan, Fig. 19)

b to middle (southeast) corner of temple (B on the plan)

c to right corner of pedestal S; right (northeast) corner of temple (C on the plan)

d to left corner of monument M

e to left corner of altar steps* (C' on the plan); right corner of monument M

f to left corner of monument N; right corner of altar steps

g to right corner of monument N.

ANGLES OF VISION FROM POINT A

Angle $ac = 60° = 180°/3$.
Angle $cd = 30° = 180°/6$.
Angle $dg = 60° = 180°/3$.

Angle ac is subdivided as follows: angle $ab = 36°$, and angle $bc = 24°$; i.e., angle ac is subdivided in a ratio of $3:2$.

DISTANCES FROM POINT A

A is equidistant from the southeast corner of the temple (B) and the southwest corner of the altar base (B'), i.e., 11.30 m.

A is equidistant from the northeast corner of the temple (C) and the northwest corner of the altar (C'), i.e., 25.60 m (possibly 50 Egyptian ells; see Chapter 3, note 4).

A is equidistant from the southwest corner of the temple (D'') and a point (D) on the northern terrace wall, i.e., 38.55 m (possibly 75 Egyptian ells).

The distance from A to the northeast corner of the temple (C) is therefore $2/3$ AD, because $AC/DD = 25.60/38.55 = 2/3$.

In other words, construction of the equilateral triangle $AD''D$ determines the position of the enclosure wall.

FIELD OF VISION FROM POINT A

From point A, there were two equal fields of vision, to right and left, each 60°, separated by an open view down the center, 30°. The paved path from altar to temple was too low to affect this. The view to the left exactly encompassed the temple within an angle of 60°. To the right, the complex of monument M, the altar, and monument N again fell within a 60° angle. The spectator thus saw two completely symmetrical masses to right and left from a narrow central line of vision, 30°, whose open view followed the direct axis of the propylon.

A mathematical symmetry exists, but it is a visual symmetry, relating to the building masses as seen from this point, not as they actually exist. The most important relationship is the ratio $2:1:2$ (building mass, free space, building mass). But the ratio 3:2 also determines the organization of the space, e.g., the relationship of the two sides of the temple and the distances seen from A to its left and right corners. These relationships between angles and sight lines determine the disposition of all buildings and monuments in the precinct; they are based on a division of the space into six parts and follow conditions laid down by the equilateral triangle $AD''D$. If the Ionic votive column (E) still existed at this time, it too would have been incorporated in the system, as its distance from A (AE) is equal to the height of the triangle $AD''D$. Line a is oriented to the west, and line d to the north, so that two of the most important cardinal points are stressed by a sharp line between solid and void. The axis of the propylon and the clear field of vision are both directed toward the north (15° west of north).

THE STRUCTURES

The ground plan of the temple of Aphaia has a ratio of 1:2; its dimensions (at the lowest step) are 15.50 by 30.30 m.

---

[1] I followed Furtwängler's history of this site, *Aegina: das Heiligtum der Aphaia*, Munich, 1906, but I do not entirely concur with his ground plans. Three of these are reproduced here: Figures 18, 20, 21. I drew Figure 19, on which my geometric construction is based, after comparing these three plans and checking them by sample surveys carried out on the site. Although my own plans are not executed with the utmost precision, their dimensions are more accurate than those of Furtwängler's plans, which were drawn up for other purposes and from a different point of view [i.e., they were less concerned with site relationships].
[2] Furtwängler, *Aegina: das Heiligtum der Aphaia*, p. 67.
[3] Ibid., p. 85.
[4] Ibid., p. 156.

Works Consulted by the Author
Cockerell, Charles Robert. *The Temples of Jupiter Panhellenius at Aegina and of Apollo Epicurius at Bassae.* London: Weale, 1860.

Furtwängler, Adolf. *Aegina: das Heiligtum der Aphaia.* 2 vols. Munich: Franz, 1906.

Additional References
Invernizzi, Antonio. *I frontoni del tempio di Aphaia ad Egina.* Turin: Giappichelli, 1965.

Welter, Gabriel. *Aigina.* Berlin: Mann, 1938.

17 Aegina, Sacred Precinct of Aphaia. View from
point A, 1968.

18   Aegina, Sacred Precinct of Aphaia. View,
drawn in 1901. (Furtwängler.)

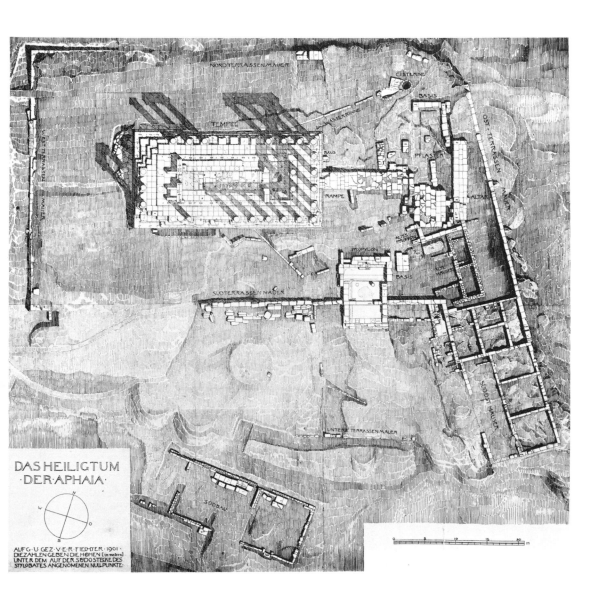

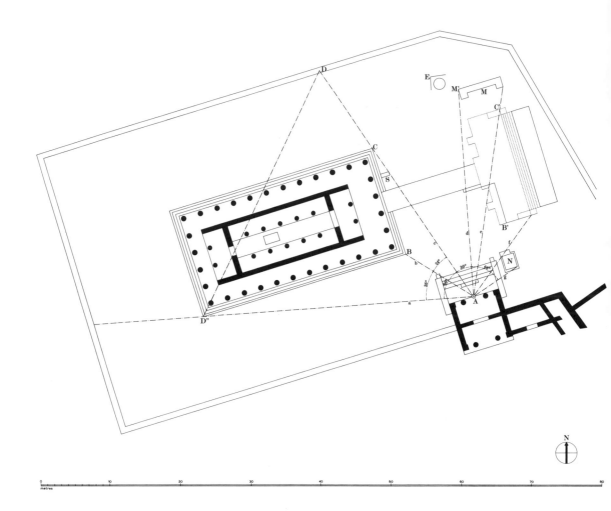

20 Aegina, Sacred Precinct of Aphaia. Plan, showing four different periods. (Furtwängler.)

21 Aegina, Sacred Precinct of Aphaia. Plan of the great altar. (Furtwängler.)

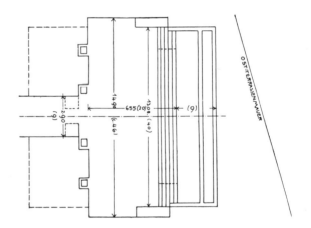

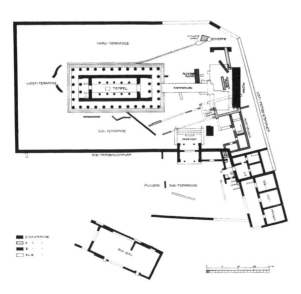

The Delphineion at Miletus, Fifth and Fourth Centuries B.C.

Basing my study on plans prepared by the excavators,[1] I examined the organization of the layout of the Delphineion at four different periods: Delphineion I, fifth and fourth centuries B.C.; Delphineion II, third and second centuries B.C.; Delphineion III, first century B.C. and first century A.D.; Delphineion IV, after the first century A.D.

Nothing is definitely known of the original form or layout of the Delphineion.[2] From the existing ruins it appears that it was first built on this site when Miletus was refounded shortly after 479 B.C. The first Delphineion occupied only about half the area of the later one; it was the size of one of the city blocks and was surrounded by roads (Fig. 23). According to Gerkan, it is not possible to accept that the altar base formed part of the earliest altar, dating from before the Persian invasion, although the existing base does show signs of the altar having been reconstructed.[3]

In the time of Alexander the Great, the Delphineion was redeveloped, and the precinct was more than doubled in size through the addition of a large horseshoe-shaped stoa. The various monuments shown in Figure 24 date from the early Hellenistic period.

The erection of a western stoa (Fig. 26) marked yet another stage of development.[4] Although its exact date is unknown, it could not have been built before the late Hellenistic period. There is no clear evidence as to whether the central tholos was built in Hellenistic or Roman times.[5] I have shown it in my plan of the late Hellenistic period (Fig. 26); Gerkan believed this date to be the most likely, although in the official publication of the excavations the question is left open.

The Delphineion underwent a third radical transformation in the early Roman period (at the end of the first or beginning of the second century A.D.), when it was surrounded on all four sides by a reconstructed Roman stoa (Fig. 27).

From the inscriptions on the structures still extant, we realize that the sacred precinct must have been embellished with very many more inscribed monuments. There are now very few remains from which one can gain a notion of the richness of its former state,[6] but fortunately enough structures have survived to enable us to make important observations regarding the organization of the layout.

Delphineion I, after 479 B.C.

Organization of the Site. An entrance is presumed in the center of the west wall of the Delphineion (Fig. 23), and point B is located in the middle of its inner face.

SIGHT LINES FROM POINT B

a to right corner of the northern stoa

b to left (northern) side of the great central altar

c to right corner of the great central altar

d to left corner of the southern stoa

ANGLES OF VISION FROM POINT B

The angle between the left-hand part of the western wall of the Delphineion and line $a = 61° = 180°/3$.

Angle $ad = 58° = 180°/3$.

The angle between line d and the right-hand part of the western wall $= 61° = 180°/3$.

DISTANCES FROM POINT B

If a semicircle with radius 15.20 m (x) is described from B, it passes through the following points:

the west corner of the northern stoa

the southeast corner of the great central altar

the outermost of a row of three circular altars

the west corner of the southern stoa.

We also find that the length of lines a and d, extending from B to the farther corners of the northern and southern stoas, is equal and measures 30.80 m (y).

Hence $2x = y$.

The distance of 30.80 m may be taken as equivalent to 100 Attic feet, as used in Athens before the Persian invasion.[7] The central altar is set

[54]

slightly diagonally in the space, so that the line of its northern side, if projected, would meet the western wall of the Delphineion at a point slightly south of B. One may perhaps be justified in believing that this was done so that the northeast corner of the altar would be clearly visible from B, for it is this corner that is at the critical distance from B of 15.20 m (x).

Delphineion II after 334 B.C.

Organization of the Site. In the reconstruction of the Delphineion (Fig. 24), which was begun in 334 B.C., careful respect was paid to all existing monuments. There were three entrances, all in the western wall. Points A, B, and C lie in the middle of each opening, on the line of the inner face of the wall.

SIGHT LINES FROM POINT C

a to left tangent of the large west-facing exedra
b to right corner of the small south-facing exedra
d to left corner of the north-facing exedra
e to right tangent of a cylindrical pedestal; right corner of the great central altar; right corner of the inscribed stele
f to left corner of the square pedestal
g to right corner of the same square pedestal; left tangent of the nearest of the row of three circular altars. The field between lines *b* and *d* is left open.

SIGHT LINES FROM POINT B

b to left corner of the inscribed stele
c to right corner of the south-facing exedra
d to left corner of the large west-facing exedra
e to right corner of the great central altar; left corner of the north-facing exedra
f to right corner of the inscribed stele.

The field between lines *c* and *d* is free of structures. All the features noted at Delphineion I, as seen from point B, still exist.

SIGHT LINES FROM POINT A

a to left corner of the great central altar
b to right corner of the square pedestal; right corner of the great central altar; right corner of the south-facing exedra

c to left tangent of the most northerly of the three circular altars; left corner of the inscribed stele; left corner of the north-facing exedra
d to right tangent of the most southerly of the three circular altars; left tangent of the circular fountain at the far end of the enclosure.

The field between lines *b* and *c* is free of structures.

The diagonals of the enclosure divide the area into two identical right-angled triangles, each with one angle of 60° and the other of 30° (180°/3 and 180°/6). Line *b* from point C and line *c* from point A not only run parallel to these diagonals but also determine the two open fields of vision; they are therefore the most important sight lines from each of these two entrances. During the period of Delphineion I the entire space was organized within an angle of 60° from point B. With the enlargement of the precinct this organization was no longer possible from point B, but the space was divided upon the same principle from the new entrances C and A.

During the erection of the south-facing exedra it proved necessary to remove an earlier pedestal (A in Fig. 25). In the account of the excavations the following explanation is given for the selection of this position for the exedra: "The reason for the choice of this particular location can most easily be explained by the care in the placing of the south-facing exedra symmetrically opposite the north-facing one, which is consequently thought to have been constructed rather earlier."[8] But, as the matter of symmetry is not taken into account in the relations between the great central altar, the large west-facing exedra, and the north-facing exedra, it seems unlikely that it would have become so important in determining the position of the south-facing exedra: this can be explained by the importance of the sight line *b* from the already existing entrance C, which the new exedra would have to respect.

Delphineion III, Late Hellenistic Period
Organization of the Site. The construction of a
stoa along the western wall did not materially
alter the organization of the precinct. The entrances remained the same, and the most important lines of vision were carefully preserved.
The central tholos (as mentioned earlier, we
cannot be certain that it was erected at this
time) is encompassed by lines b and c at 60°
from entrances C and A, and its presence
strengthens the importance of these sightlines.
All other features noted at Delphineion II still
remain.

Delphineion IV, after First Century A.D.
Organization of the Site. In the early Roman
period, about 100 A.D., the Delphineion was
again reconstructed. In rebuilding the stoas,
even greater emphasis was given to the two
chief sightlines b and c from the entrances C
and A, since the two farthest corners of the enclosure were now sited directly upon them. The
entire central tholos could be seen within an
angle of 15° from each of these entrances (i.e.,
180°/12) between the columns of the western
stoa. This leads me to believe that the central
tholos belongs to this early Roman layout
rather than to the late Hellenistic one, but, as I
have said, this cannot be stated definitely. Two
other assumptions seem equally probable: first,
that the tholos and the new stoas were planned
at the same time, but, for unknown reasons,
only the tholos was actually built; second, that
the stoas were both planned and constructed
after the tholos had been built and that their
form was derived as a result of consideration
for the existing sightlines.

(Notes to pages 54–56 are on page 63.)

22 Miletus, Delphineion. View from the west, circa 1914. (Kawerau and Rehm.)

23 Miletus, Delphineion I, fifth and fourth centuries B.C. Plan.

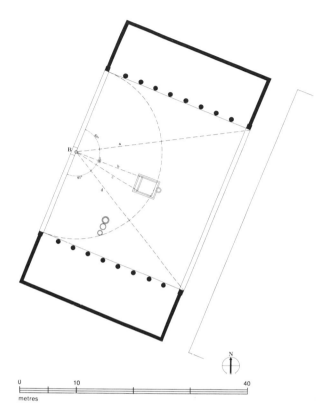

24   Miletus, Delphineion II, third and second centuries B.C. Plan.

25   Miletus, Delphineion II. Plan of detail.

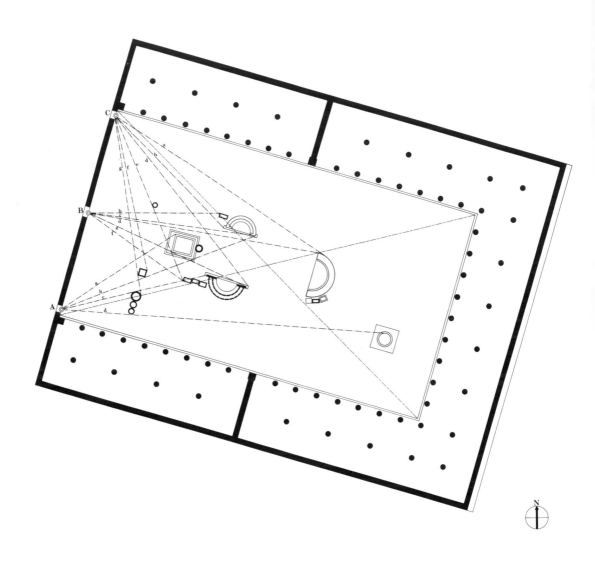

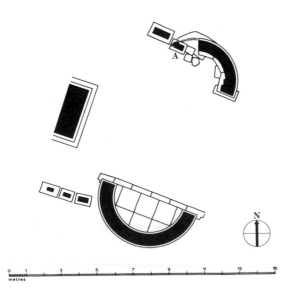

26 Miletus, Delphineion III, first century B.C. and
first century A.D. Plan.

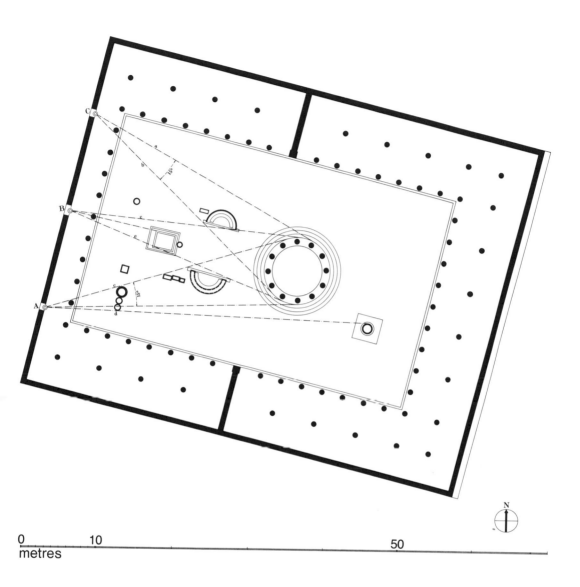

0   10   50
metres

[59]

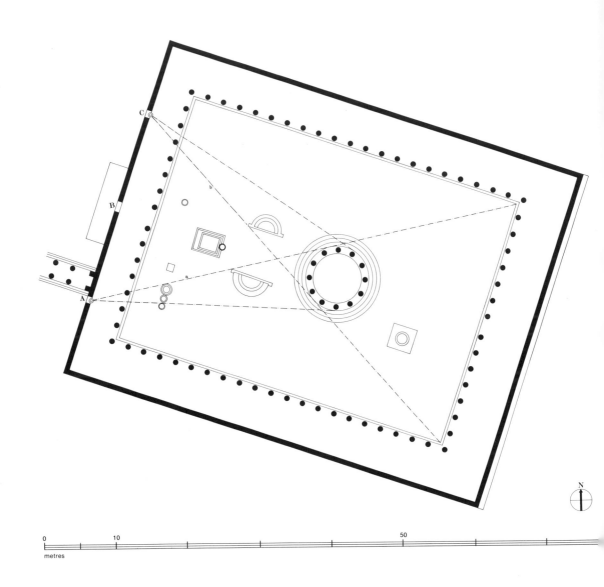

28 Miletus, Delphineion III. Reconstruction.
(Kawerau and Rehm.)

29 Miletus, Delphineion. Composite plan.
(Kawerau and Rehm.)

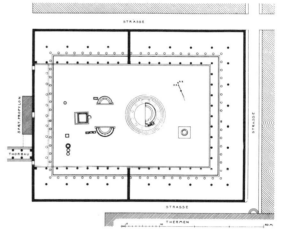

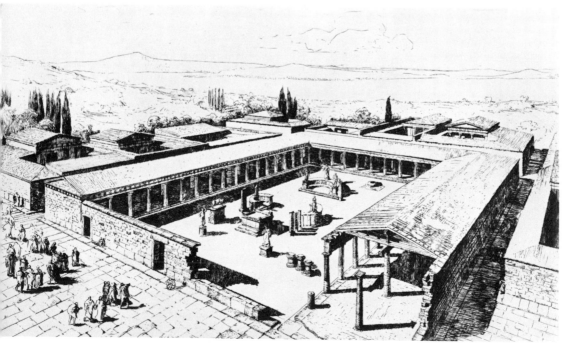

The Agora at Miletus, Fifth Century B.C. to Second Century A.D.

A complete survey of the architectural development of the agora at Miletus would be beyond the scope of this work. Many public buildings were frequently altered and enlarged during the seven centuries of the city's existence, from the fifth century B.C. to the second century A.D. I have therefore confined my study to the four chief periods examined by the excavators.[9] A plan is given for each period (Figs. 31, 32, 35, 36) so that comparison can be made of the layout of the site at each of these four phases of development.

Agora I, Fifth and Fourth Centuries B.C.
Organization of the Site. At this period it is possible to reconstruct only the northern part of the agora (Fig. 31). According to the excavators, "The ground plan of the stoa complex indicates that the extension of the later agora was not yet contemplated."[10] We should therefore consider the layout at this period as a complete entity, not as the first stage in a development. No traces remain of definite entrances from the city into this area. The layout of the southern part of the site is uncertain: it probably consisted of a large rectangle within which several small monuments were located, but the exact positions of these are still unknown.

Agora II, Second Century B.C.
Organization of the Site. By the middle of the second century B.C. the agora had acquired its final, typically Hellenistic form (Fig. 32). Earlier buildings had been gradually completed, a new southern agora had been built, and the area just south of the northern entrance had been reorganized. As in the first phase, this layout does not show signs of being developed according to a prearranged plan;[11] it should be considered as having evolved from the already existing layout and as independent of later development.

It was only at the end of the second century B.C. that an eastern boundary wall was built enclosing the northern agora and cutting the formed space into two parts. This area could be entered from several of the city streets, but the

most important entrance was doubtless the one from the southern agora (*B* on the plan, Fig. 32) as this provided access for almost all the traffic from the southern part of the city (Fig. 33). Two of the other entrances are marked *C* and *D* on the plan (Fig. 32).

SIGHT LINES FROM POINT *B*
Point *B* lies in the center of the opening between two stoas on the line of their northern façades.
a to right corner of monument *M* on the plan (Fig. 32); left corner of the propylon in the center of the new boundary wall
b to right corner of the stoa facing the harbor; left corner of the city block nearest the harbor
c to left corner of monument *M'* on the plan; left corner of the Delphineion
d to left corner of monument *M"* on the plan; right corner of the propylon to the eastern building
e to right corner of monument *M"*; entrance *D* on the plan.

SIGHT LINES FROM POINT *C*
f to left corner of monument *M'* on the plan; right corner of the Council House
g to left corner of monument *M"* on the plan; right corner of the propylon in the new boundary wall
h to right corner of monument *M"* on the plan; right corner of the propylon to the eastern building

SIGHT LINES FROM POINT *D*
i to left corner of monument *M"* on the plan; entrance *B*
j to right corner of monument *M"* on the plan; right corner of monument *M'* on the plan; left corner of the propylon to the Council House
k to left corner of the propylon to the eastern building; left corner of the eastern building; right corner of monument *M* on the plan.

Sight lines drawn from the other entrances yield similar results.

The newly enclosed northern agora could be entered only from the propylon, which lay di-

[62]

rectly on the axis of the temple. But lines *l* and *m* seem to indicate the position of another entrance (*E*), as from point *D* the propylon would be seen in its entirety between two monuments. This entrance is also denoted by the later erection in the middle of the agora of a small altar (*F* on the plan), which is so placed that it in no way interferes with the view of all existing structures from point *E*. In fact, line *n*, which runs from point *E* to the right corner of the altar, also touches the left corner of the last of these structures, thus bringing the altar into the picture as part of a continuous sequence of objects, with no gaps or overlapping. It seems, therefore, that the position of the altar (*F*) was determined by the axis of the agora and line *n* from point *E*.

If we assume that point *E* represents an entrance to the agora, then it must also have been a point of access from the harbor or from an important space, such as a temple precinct. The space to the north is sufficiently large for either assumption to be possible, although neither is certain. Gerkan considered it probable that point *E* represents an entrance either from the harbor or from an earlier important architectural complex.

Agora III, First Century B.C. and First Century A.D.

Organization of the Site. At the beginning of the Christian era the general layout of the site remained substantially as before, but the desire to create enclosed spaces was manifest everywhere (Fig. 35). The continued respect for the freedom of sight line *n* adds strength to the supposition that an entrance existed at point *E*, but this still cannot be confirmed.

Agora IV, Second Century A.D.

Organization of the site. By the second century A.D. the site had become completely Romanized through the erection of new stoas that cut across many of the earlier sight lines from the entrances (Fig. 36).

[1] Published in the series *Milet: Ergebnisse der Ausgrabungen*, ed. Theodor Wiegand. I verified these at the site. My own plans shown here in Figures 23–26 are based on plates 23–26 in volume 1, part 6, of this series: Armin von Gerkan, *Der Nordmarkt und der Hafen an der Löwenbucht.*
[2] Armin von Gerkan, *Griechische Städteanlagen*, Berlin, 1924, p. 38.
[3] Ibid., p. 40.
[4] Georg Kawerau and Albert Rehm, *Das Delphinion in Milet*, Milet: Ergebnisse der Ausgrabungen, vol. 1, pt. 3, p. 141.
[5] Ibid., pp. 147–148.
[6] Gerkan, *Griechische Städteanlagen*, p. 39.
[7] [See Chapter 3, note 4, for discussion of Greek feet.]
[8] *Milet: Ergebnisse der Ausgrabungen*, vol. 1, pt. 3, p. 150.
[9] After studying the layouts published in *Milet*, particularly those in *Der Nordmarkt und der Hafen an der Löwenbucht*, by Gerkan, I visited the site and found that my interpretations were confirmed.
[10] Gerkan, *Der Nordmarkt und der Hafen an der Löwenbucht*, p. 91.
[11] Ibid., p. 92.

Works Consulted by the Author
Berlin, Staatliche Museen. *Milet: Ergebnisse der Ausgrabungen und Untersuchungen seit dem Jahre 1899*, edited by Theodor Wiegand. Berlin, 1906–1926. (I referred especially to Armin von Gerkan, *Der Nordmarkt und der Hafen an der Löwenbucht*, 1922, and Georg Kawerau and Albert Rehm, *Das Delphinion in Milet*, 1914.)

Gerkan, Armin von. *Griechische Städteanlagen*. Berlin: De Gruyter, 1924.

Additional References
Kobylina, M. M. *Milet*. Moscow, 1965.

Weickert, Carl. "Neue Ausgrabungen in Milet." In *Neue deutsche Ausgrabungen im Mittelmeergebiet und im vorderen Orient*. Berlin: Deutsches Archäologisches Institut, 1959, pp. 181–196.

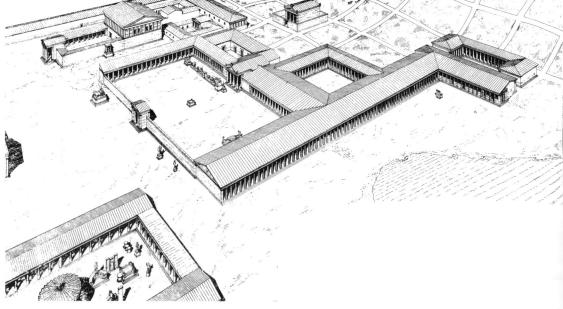

31 Miletus, Agora I, fifth and fourth centuries B.C.
Plan.

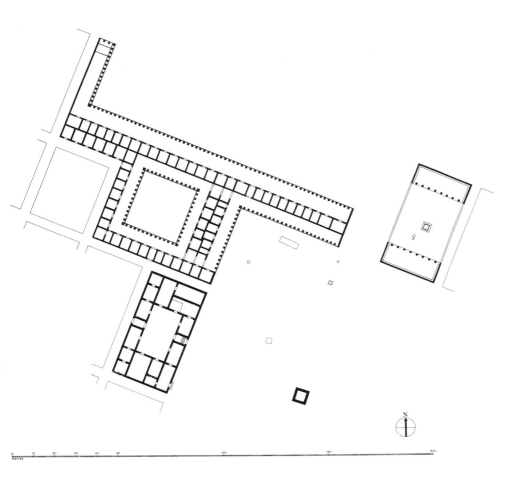

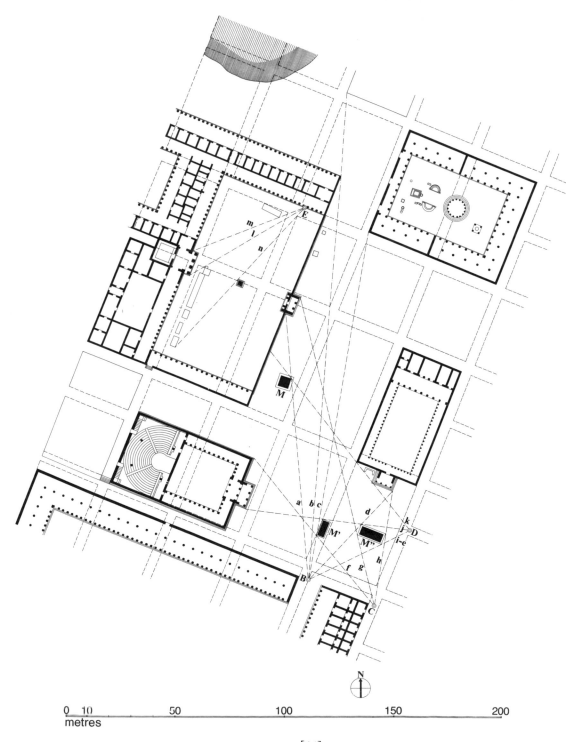

0   10   50   100   150   200
metres

33 Miletus. General plan. (Gerkan.)   34 Miletus. Plan of city center. (Gerkan.)

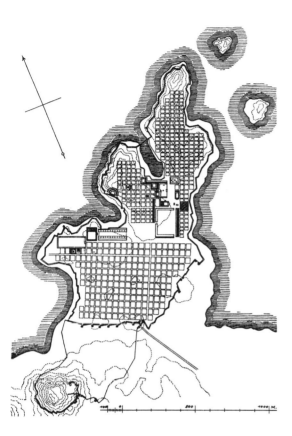

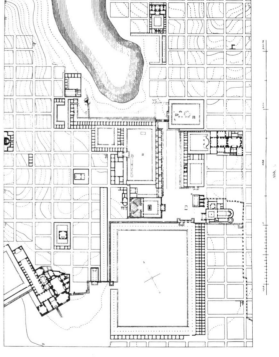

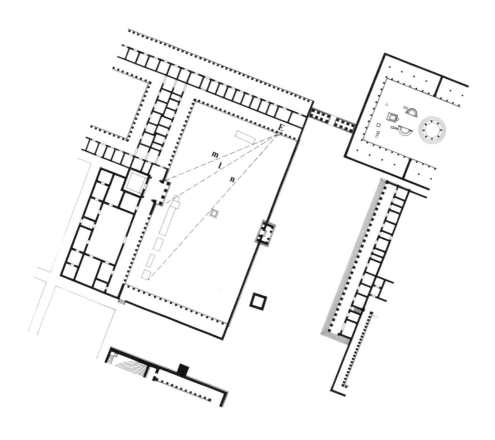

0 10   50   100   150
metres

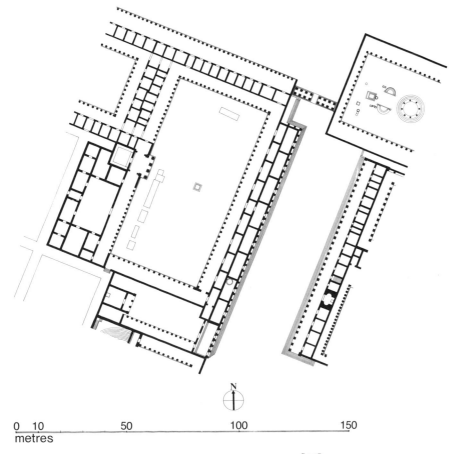

N

0   10   50   100   150
metres

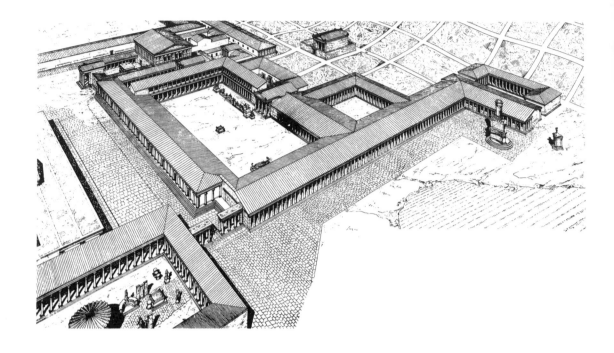

The Altis at Olympia, Fifth Century B.C.

The large enclosure, or Altis, at Olympia was one of the earliest Greek sanctuaries.[1] Its many buildings date from several different periods, and the layout cannot be considered as representing an organized plan (Fig. 41). In fact, the Altis is a typical example of a site that has continually been enriched by the addition of new buildings and monuments—in this case, from the earliest archaic period to late Roman times, and even into the Christian era.

The existing foundations of buildings and monuments are insufficient to permit a reconstruction of the form of the early precinct, especially as the original lines of its enclosure walls and entrances have not yet been traced. Only after the rebuilding of the temple of Zeus in the fifth century B.C. can there be some degree of certainty. It is possible that a general reorganization of the site was undertaken at that time and that careful heed was paid to the existing monuments. By the time the new temple of Zeus was completed, the Altis had acquired a fully organized layout containing the following structures:

the temple of Zeus, built between 470 and 456 B.C.

the Heraion, probably the oldest building on the site (the early temple with wooden columns was rebuilt in stone about the beginning of the sixth century B.C.)

several treasuries, sixth century B.C. onward

the Prytaneion, fifth century B.C.

the first Echo Stoa, rebuilt in the second half of the fourth century B.C.

the Pelopion, first planned as a circular precinct sacred to Pelops and later given a pentagonal enclosure wall

the Hippodameion, of which no definite traces remain, but whose outline I have sketched in, based on the system that I have described

the altar of Zeus, of which there are no definite remains

the altar of Hera, the date of which is undetermined

many small altars and votive structures of various periods.

The form given to the enclosure at this time remained substantially unchanged for a century, as the main lines of the layout were retained when the following new structures were added in the fourth century B.C.:

the southeast building, constructed in the first half of the fourth century B.C. and destroyed by Nero's building in the first century A.D.

the new Echo Stoa, second half of the fourth century B.C.

the Metroon, temple of the Mother of the Gods, first half of the fourth century B.C.

the circular Philippeion, begun shortly after 338 B.C. by Philip II of Macedon

numerous new altars and votive structures.

The principles on which the layout was organized remained identical during both these periods (the first of which was distinctly classic, and the second, distinctly Hellenistic) even though the site acquired many new buildings during the fourth century. Throughout both periods also, the boundaries and especially the entrances to the Altis remained unchanged. Because of the similarity between the two periods, I shall discuss them together.

During the Roman period, which I treat separately, the Altis was repeatedly altered and extended: new stoas were built, some of the entrances were changed, and the exedra of Herodus Atticus was cut into the northern boundary.

The Classical and Hellenistic Altis, Fifth and Fourth Centuries B.C.

Organization of the Site. There were four entrances (A, B, C, and E on the plan, Fig. 39). The organization of the site will be discussed as seen from each of these in turn. No traces have been found of a pre-Roman southeast entrance at point A. I have therefore assumed that, as was customary elsewhere, the Roman portal was built where the Greek entrance gate had formerly been situated; this would have marked the end of the sacred way and the beginning of the Altis. This assumption is supported by our knowledge that in ancient Greek times the main road ended at approximately this point. The position of the southwest entrance, just below point B, is definitely established. On entering the Altis from this entrance and moving in the most important direction, that is, toward the altars of Zeus and Hera, one must pass close to the northwest corner of the temple of Zeus. I thus consider that this point (D on the plan) could also have become an important starting point for the layout of the west side of the precinct. Entrance C in the northwest corner of the Altis is not entirely certain, but I have accepted the position determined by the excavators in their reconstruction of the site. Although the position of entrance E in the southern wall is well established, it seems to have had very little significance in the organization of the site plan.

As the analysis will show, the field of vision from each of these points consists of a central opening bounded on either side by a continuous series of structures. The position, orientation, and distance of the buildings from each point are determined on the basis of the 30° angle. Throughout, one can sense the desire to connect the outlines of the different structures with one another and with the lines of the landscape, to form a continuous unity, and within this unity to emphasize one opening: one clear and unobstructed path leading out into the landscape. That this was the general purpose seems certain. With regard to the details, however, because of the complexity of the site and the need for consideration of the many existing structures at every new stage of development it was inevitable that in some instances the relationships established should be only approximately correct.

SIGHT LINES FROM POINT A

Measurements taken at the site show that point A (Fig. 39) is on the axis of the Roman entry, one meter back from the inner edge of the Roman foundations.

(* indicates that the exact position of these structures is uncertain.)

a to left (southwest) corner of the temple of Zeus; middle (southeast) corner of the Theocoleon, the priests' residence outside the Altis (see Fig. 41).

b to left side of the Victory of Paeonios; right (northeast) corner of the temple of Zeus (F on the plan)

c to right side of the Victory statue; left (southwest) corner of the Heraion (M on the plan)

d to left corner of the altar of Zeus*;[2] right (northeast) corner of the Heraion

e to right corner of the altar of Zeus*; left corner of the altar of Hera

f to right corner of the altar of Hera

g to left end of the series of altars and treasuries on the upper terrace

h to left (southwest) corner of the Metroon (G on the plan); right corner of the first treasury

i to right (northeast) corner of the Metroon; left corner of the propylon of the Hippodameion*

j to left corner of the nearest monument

k to left (northwest) corner of the Hellenistic Echo Stoa

l to right corner of the nearest monument; left corner of the nearest altar

m to right corner of the façade of the Hellenistic Echo Stoa (southwest corner)

n to left corner of the southeast building; right (southeast) corner of the Hellenistic Echo Stoa.

[72]

(This was the right, i.e., southwest, corner of the façade of the former stoa.)

ANGLES OF VISION FROM POINT A

Angle $ab = 31°$ ($30° = 180°/6$).
Angle $bh = 30° = 180°/6$.
Angle $hk = 30° = 180°/6$.
Angle $km = 30° = 180°/6$.

The entire field of vision is encompassed within an angle of $121°$ ($120° = 2 \times 180°/3$). If we examine the angles that encompass each of the major buildings we find
the Heraion lies within an angle of $15° = 180°/12$;
the Metroon lies within an angle of $10° - 180°/18 = 1/3(180°/6)$;
the Echo Stoa lies within an angle of $30° = 180°/6$;
the temple of Zeus lies within an angle of $31° =$ ca. $180°/6$.

It is noteworthy that the Parthenon at Athens, which has certain similarities with the temple of Zeus, also falls within an angle of $30°$ when viewed from the propylon.

DISTANCES FROM POINT A

If an equilateral triangle AFF' is described on the base AF (F is the northeast corner of the temple of Zeus; see Fig. 39), we find that F' falls along the line k, and that the sides of the triangle measure 80.5 m, or approximately 250 Olympian feet ($250 \times 0.328 = 82.0$ m).[3] If an arc is described from point A with radius AF (80.5 m), the point at which it crosses line i may indicate the left corner of the propylon to the Hippodameion. If the triangle AFF' is inverted on its side FF' to form the triangle FGF', we find that G falls on line h at the southwest corner of the Metroon.

Hence $AG = 2\,AF\sqrt{3}/2 = AF\sqrt{3}$
or $AG = 80.5 \times 1.732 = 139.4$ m.
Measurements taken on the site show that $AG = 139.2$ m.
In other words, the significant measurements are $x : x\sqrt{3}$. It may also be noted that the basic dimension used in the reorganization of the Acropolis at Athens, which was roughly contemporary with the Olympian Altis, was 79.6 m; this is very near the dimension 80.5 m that we find in the Altis.

FIELD OF VISION FROM POINT A

From left to right, we see from point A (Fig. 40)
the temple of Zeus
the Victory of Paeonios
the Heraion
the altar of Zeus
the altar of Hera
an open field of vision looking toward the small Hill of Gaia[4]
a fountain (very low and perhaps not visible), some altars, and the first treasury
the Metroon
the Hill of Kronos with the Hippodameion below it
the Echo Stoa.

The differing orientation of these buildings and the distances between them are determined by the equilateral triangle AFF', in particular the angle of $30°$ ($180°/6$), or a twelfth part of the total field of $360°$.

Figure 40 shows how the mass of the temple of Zeus is balanced symmetrically by the Hill of Kronos, and the Metroon by the Heraion. Both are symmetrically placed on either side of the axis leading to the small Hill of Gaia, which rises only slightly higher than the Heraion and the Metroon. This axial symmetry is clearly strengthened by two balancing groves of trees, one within the Pelopion to the left, and the other in the Hippodameion to the right.

The Victory statue was apparently placed to occupy exactly the small angle of vision between the northeast corner of the temple of Zeus and the southwest corner of the Heraion, perhaps to emphasize the difference in volume of these two buildings. Its position is very similar to that of the statue of Athena Promachos on the Acropolis at Athens, which, when seen from the Propylaea, stands exactly between the Erechtheion and the smaller mass of the altar of Athena (Fig. 2). The top of the statue of Victory and the tip of the acroterion on the temple of Zeus were on the same horizontal level. This may also have been intentional.

It seems clear that a principal aim of this symmetrically organized layout, in which the landscape is incorporated, was to maintain the importance of the central axial opening. This marks the processional route of the people through the sacred precinct from entrance A to the altars. Also, from this entrance the peak of the Hill of Kronos lies directly to the north. Thus, one of the cardinal compass points is made an integral part of the composition.

Although this is the only instance in which we have found a spatially symmetrical layout, the conscious use of symmetry by the Greeks is not precluded. They did not shun symmetry when its use suited their purpose. For example, on leaving the Altis through entrance A, going directly south, one has the impression that the landscape ahead opens up axially and symmetrically. The broad band of the river Alpheios lies directly across the path, and the background is occupied by a balanced line of hills, the tallest in the center and two lower ones on either side (Fig. 42). The outline of this mountain chain, which dominates the whole valley, is immediately impressive. This was felt by the ancient Greeks and re-echoed in their layout. The outline of the mountains is still visible today, but the view of the river is now obstructed by alluvial deposits; one must imagine it stretching in a straight line across the foreground.

SIGHT LINES FROM POINT B

(* indicates that the exact position of these structures is uncertain.)

Point B (Fig. 43) has been located a short way in from the entrance, since the position of the monument immediately to the right of the entrance would have impeded a clear view of the temple of Zeus. Figure 46 shows a perspective view of the Altis from this point.

a to left tangent of the Philippeion

b to right tangent of the Philippeion; left corner of the entry to the Prytaneion

c to left side of the small altar before the Heraion; right corner of the entry to the Prytaneion

d to left (southwest) corner of the Heraion, approximately along the line of the west façade

e to left corner of the propylon to the Pelopion; west side of the Pelopion*

f to right (northeast) corner of the propylon to the Pelopion (H on the plan)

g to right (southeast) corner of the Heraion

h to right (northwest) corner of the temple of Zeus (D on the plan); left corner of the first of the row of treasuries on the upper terrace

i to right (southeast) corner of the temple of Zeus (H' on the plan)

j to left side of the Victory statue; right corner of the Echo Stoa*

k to right side of the Victory statue; left corner of the southeast building.

ANGLES OF VISION FROM POINT B

Angle $af = 30° = 180°/6$.

Angle $fi = 60° = 180°/3$.

DISTANCES FROM POINT B

From point B, an equilateral triangle BHH' can be formed, with H lying on line f at the corner of the propylon to the Pelopion and H' lying on line i at the southeast corner of the temple of Zeus, the sides measuring 88.0 m.

The distance from point B to point I—the ramp to the propylon of the Pelopion—measures 76.2 m.

Hence $BI = BH \sqrt{3}/2 =$ the height of the equilateral triangle BHH'.

This implies that the significant measurements from this point were $y : y\sqrt{3} : 2y$.

Distances to other important points from point B cannot be precisely determined without a more accurate field survey. When studied on the existing plans they show small deviations

[74]

from the usual system that cannot be explained without more complete information.

FIELD OF VISION FROM POINT B

Figure 46 shows the view from point B during the first period, before the construction of the Philippeion in the first half of the fourth century B.C.

From left to right we see

the Philippeion

the Prytaneion

the Heraion, with the propylon to the Pelopion appearing in the center of its façade, giving the impression that this axial and symmetrical position was intentional

an open field of vision between the Heraion and the temple of Zeus, toward the Hill of Kronos

the temple of Zeus

the Echo Stoa

the statue of Victory of Paeonios

the southeast building, to the extreme right and closing the picture.

Seen from point B the Victory statue exactly occupies the space between the Echo Stoa and the southeast building. Just as when viewed from point A, its height is related to the temple of Zeus, although in a different way: from point A it emphasizes the upward thrust of the temple summit; from point B it punctuates the far end of the long pediment.

The outline of the Hill of Kronos appears to continue on the line of the architrave of the temple of Zeus and to link it with the Heraion. The hill on the left and the Victory statue on the right thus form a visual unity with the temple of Zeus.

From point B the north point lies directly along line d, which leads to the west end of the Heraion, so that this principal direction is again emphasized in the layout.

SIGHT LINES FROM POINT D

Point D (Fig. 43) lies at the extreme northwest corner of the temple of Zeus, at the corner of the steps, between lines g and h from point B.

a to left (southwest) corner of the Heraion

b to right (southeast) corner of the Heraion

c to right (southeast) corner of the Pelopion (in Roman times [Fig. 49] this line ran along the southeast wall of the enclosure)

d to left (northwest) corner of the Metroon; right corner of the third treasury on the upper terrace

e to right (southeast) corner of the Metroon; left corner of the great altar on the upper terrace

f to left (northwest) corner of the Echo Stoa; left corner of the last treasury on the upper terrace.

ANGLES OF VISION FROM POINT D

The only statement that can be made with certainty is that the Metroon is seen within an angle of 10°, just as from point A. The other angles would need to be checked after completion of an accurate site survey.

SIGHT LINES FROM POINT C

I have placed point C (Fig. 39) in the center of the entrance determined by the excavators, on a line with the inner side of the wall enclosing the precinct.

a to left corner of the entrance to the Prytaneion

b to right (east) corner of the Prytaneion; left (northeast) corner of the Heraion

c to right side of the small altar in front of the Heraion; right (southwest) corner of the Heraion (M on plan)

d to central (northwest) corner of the Pelopion; left (northeast) corner of the temple of Zeus

e to left (northeast) corner of the propylon of the Pelopion; fifth column from the northeast corner of the temple of Zeus

f to right (southwest) corner of the propylon to the Pelopion; fifth column from the northwest corner of the temple of Zeus

g to right (southwest) corner of the temple of Zeus, before the erection of the Philippeion

h to right tangent of the Philippeion.

[75]

ANGLES OF VISION FROM POINT C

The Heraion is seen within an angle of
$30° = 180°/6$.

DISTANCES FROM POINT C

The distance from C to the far side of the entrance to the Prytaneion (K on the plan) is equal to the distance to the nearest point of the Philippeion (K' on the plan).

$CK = CK' = 20.9$ m.

Similarly, the distance to the nearest corner of the Heraion (L on the plan) is equal to the distance to the farthest point of the Philippeion (L' on the plan).

$CL = CL' = 35.5$ m.

The distance from C to the right (southwest) corner of the Heraion measures 41.6 m.

Hence $CK = CM/2$.

Arithmetically, $CK = 20.9 = 41.8/2$ (by measurement $CM = 41.6$ m).

Similarly, $CL = (\sqrt{3}/2)CM$.

Arithmetically, $CL = 35.5 = (\sqrt{3}/2)41$ and $CM = 41.0$ m (by measurement $CM = 41.6$ m).

Therefore, CK, CL, and CM are the three sides of a right-angled triangle with angles of 30°, 60°, and 90°, CM being the longest side. Similarly, they represent one side, the height, and half the base of an equilateral triangle with sides of 41.6 m. In other words, they represent a twelve-part division of the total field of 360°.

FIELD OF VISION FROM POINT C

Standing at point C (Fig. 48), looking from left to right we see

the Prytaneion

the Heraion

an open field of vision between the Heraion and the temple of Zeus

the temple of Zeus with the propylon appearing in the center of its façade, just as, from point B, the propylon had appeared in the center of the Heraion

(the Philippeion, at a later date).

The outline of the mountains in the background is linked to the outline of the temple of Zeus to form a visual unity.

SIGHT LINES FROM POINT E

As has been said, although this entrance (Fig. 43) is known to have existed, it seems to have played little part in the determination of the layout. Point E has been located in the center of the entrance on the line of the inner side of the precinct boundary wall. It is possible that the boundary line of the northeast side of the Pelopion was determined by the direction EF', F being the northeast corner of the temple of Zeus.

The Roman Altis, about 200 A.D.

Organization of the Site. In Roman times (Fig. 49) the Altis received a new boundary wall, several of the former entrances were closed, and the northwest corner, especially, was transformed by the construction of a new stoa. As a result of these changes, the earlier system of relationships ceased to exist. Moreover, the erection of the exedra of Herodus Atticus in the northern boundary wall influenced the entire site by completely blocking the open field of vision, so that the former impression of a path leading directly through the sanctuary into the landscape was utterly destroyed. The Roman Altis had become fully enclosed. Thus, many of the principles that had governed the composition of the site during the classical and Hellenistic periods—in particular, the use of the landscape as an integral part of the plan—had now been abandoned.

THE STRUCTURES

The proportions of the temple of Zeus are 1:5, and those of the Metroon, 1:2.

---

[1] Wilhelm Dörpfeld, *Alt-Olympia,* Berlin, 1935, p. 29.
[2] This is based on Hans Schleif's plan in his *Die neuen Ausgrabuugen in Olympia.*
[3] [For discussion of ancient Greek feet see Chapter 3, note 4.]
[4] [The Hill of Gaia is an offshoot of the Hill of Kronos, identified by Dörpfeld (*Alt-Olympia*, p. 63) and by Ludwig Drees (*Olympia,* pp. 12–13) as the cult center of the early "earth mother" Gaia.]

Works Consulted by the Author

Curtius, Ernst, and Adler, Friedrich. *Olympia: Die Ergebnisse der von dem deutschen Reich veranstalteten Ausgrabung.* 5 vols. Berlin: Asher, 1890–1897.

Dörpfeld, Wilhelm. *Alt-Olympia.* Berlin: Mittler, 1935.

Schleif, Hans. *Die neuen Ausgrabungen in Olympia und ihre bisherigen Ergebnisse für die antike Bauforschung.* Berlin, 1943. (The material was available for study before publication.)

Additional References

Drees, Ludwig. *Olympia.* Stuttgart: Kohlhammer, 1967.

Essen, Ausstellung, 1960. *Olympia in der Antike.* Essen, 1960.

Kontis, Ioannes D. Τό ἱερόν τῆς Ὀλυμπίας. Athens, 1958.

Schleif, Hans. *Das Philippeion.* Olympische Forschungen, edited by Emil Kunze and Hans Schleif, vol. 1. Berlin: De Gruyter, 1944.

38 Olympia, Altis. View from point A, 1969.

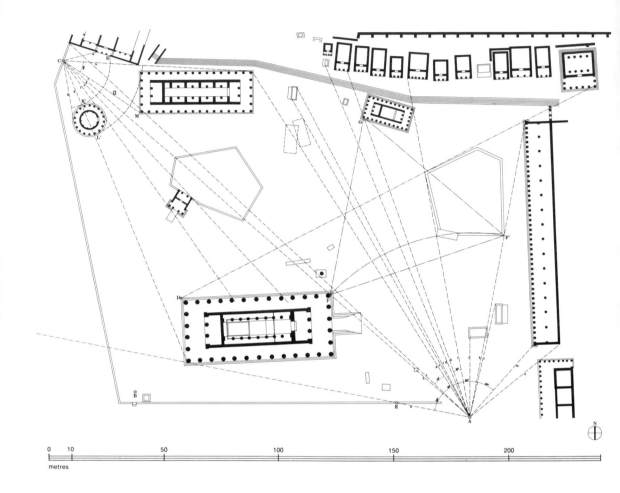

41   Olympia, Altis. General plan of the Altis and
its environment. (Curtius and Adler.)

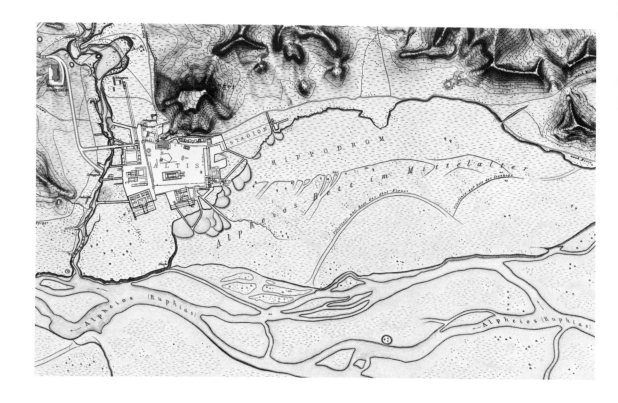

42   Olympia, Altis. View from a point east of the
treasuries, looking south, 1968.

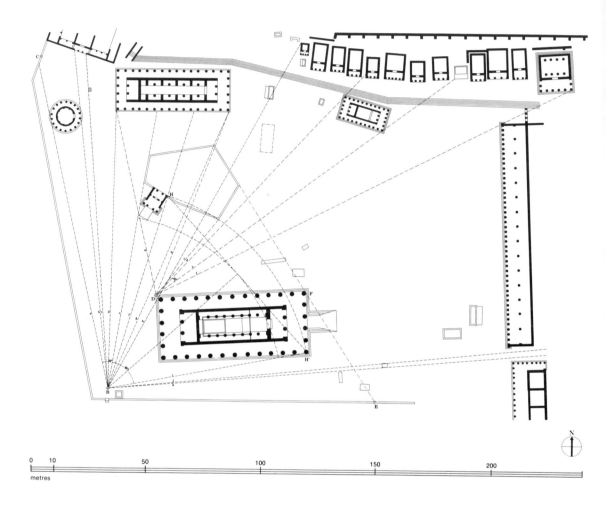

44 Olympia, Altis, Hellenistic period. Plan.
(Schleif.)

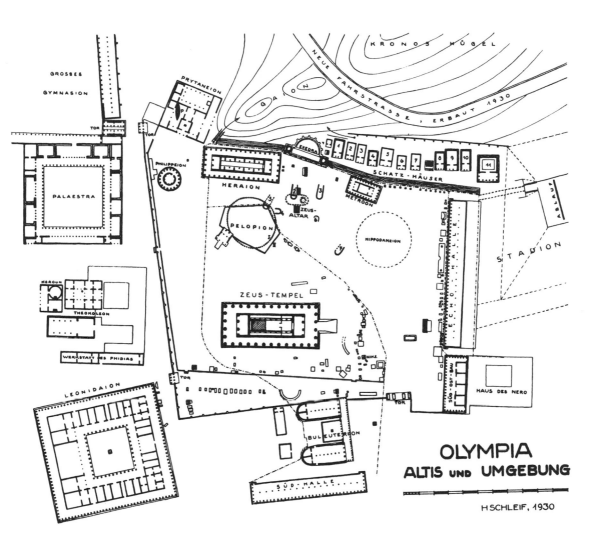

45   Olympia, Altis. View from point B, 1969.

48   Olympia, Altis. Perspective from point C.

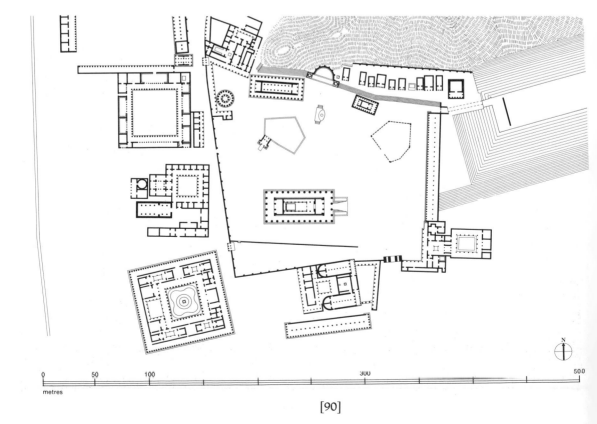

50 Olympia, Altis. Model. (Schleif.)

The Sacred Precinct of Poseidon at Sounion, Fifth Century B.C.

This temple site shows traces of two phases of active building construction. From the first phase, which dates from before the Persian invasion, there are only some remains of the early temple, built of tufa, and of the propylon. All the remains now visible seem to date from the fifth-century reconstruction: the marble temple, the north and west stoas, the marble propylon, and the altar, whose traces have been found on the rock near the southeast corner of the temple.

Remains of the layout of the earlier precinct are insufficient to permit an investigation. We know that the dimensions of the platform of the temple that lay below the present one were 30.34 × 13.12 m[1] and that those of the later marble temple were 31.15 × 13.48 m. According to Stais, an earlier tufa building lay under the fifth-century propylon, but he furnished no proof of this.[2] His opinion is supported, however, by Dörpfeld's general observation regarding the Poseidon temples that "when constructing a new building, the ancient Greek architects sometimes intentionally retained the proportions and form of an earlier building."[3] If we assume that this statement can be applied not only to the temple but to other important buildings within a sacred precinct, such as the propylon, we can perhaps justify basing the spatial layout of the fifth-century precinct at Sounion on that of the tufa temple in the archaic period.

There are various opinions about the exact date of the fifth-century marble temple. Dörpfeld considers it almost contemporary with the "Theseum" (temple of Hephaestus), beside the agora in Athens, with which it has close affinities. This would mean it is a little later than the Parthenon.[4] A probable date is about 430 B.C.[5] The large northern stoa, the small stoa, and the marble propylon all appear to have been built after the temple. Thus, while the precinct undoubtedly had an organized site plan, it is not possible to determine whether this was first created in the classical period or whether it followed lines laid down in the earlier archaic precinct that was destroyed by the Persians.

Organization of the Site about 430 B.C. The entrance was through the propylon; point A has been located on the axis of this structure at the inner edge of the platform (Fig. 52).

SIGHT LINES FROM POINT A

a to left corner (northeast) of the lowest step of the temple (B on the plan)

b to left (southeast) corner of the temple platform

c to right (northwest) corner of the temple platform

d to right (northwest) corner of the lowest step of the temple (C' on the plan)

e to left (southeast) corner of the small stoa.

ANGLES OF VISION FROM POINT A

Angle $ad = 60° = 180°/3$.

DISTANCES FROM POINT A

The distance AB along the line a to the northeast corner of the lowest step of the temple measures 27.2 m. We can call this distance x.

If we describe an equilateral triangle ABB', we find that point B' falls along the line d. If this triangle is then inverted along the side BB' to form the triangle BCB', with radius AC, we can describe an arc cutting the projection of the line AB' at C', which falls at the northwest corner of the lowest step of the temple.

Hence $AC = 2 \times AB \sqrt{3}/2 = AB \sqrt{3}$; since $AB = 27.2$, $AC = 27.2 \times 1.732 = 47.11$ m.

Measurements taken on the site show that $AC = 46.5$ m.

If another equilateral triangle ADD' is described, with its height AC, we find that point D falls close to where traces of the altar of Poseidon have been found in the rock. Thus, it is possible that point D marks the nearest (i.e., the southwest) corner of this altar, lying at a distance of $2AB$, or $2x$, from point A and upon the arc AD'.

FIELD OF VISION FROM POINT A

From left to right we can see

[92]

the eastern boundary wall of the precinct
an open field of vision
the broad-stepped base of the temple and
perhaps the altar of Poseidon
the temple of Poseidon
the stepped base of the temple
an open view of the sea
the western stoa.

The observer has two open fields of vision, one to the left of the temple, the other to the right, between the temple and the stoa. In general, we have found that whenever a sector of the field of vision is left open, it has a particular significance: it may, for instance, mark the processional way to the altars, as on the Acropolis at Athens and in the Altis at Olympia, or it may stress one of the cardinal points, as is the case, again, on the Acropolis at Athens and—where this is very clear—in the agora at Pergamon. At Sounion the open view to the left of the temple leads to the temple entrance and, most probably, to the altar of Poseidon. The open view to the right of the temple may have been left free to emphasize the path to a cave below the rock, which perhaps had special significance in the cult of Poseidon. It is also possible that this sector was not, in fact, left open but was closed by a structure of which no trace has yet been found (as was the case, for example, on the terrace of Athena at Pergamon). But, if we take the surrounding landscape into account, we cannot rule out the idea that the purpose of an open sector here was to offer an unobstructed view of the sea—the realm of Poseidon. Examination of the cardinal points of the compass reveals that the two limiting lines of this open sector to the right of the temple lie at 10° and 20° south of west, so that during the months of February and October there would be a direct view of the setting sun over the sea.

Clearly, the extension of the landscape played an important part in the plan for this precinct. The great temple is raised high in the center of the area in contrast to the other build-

ings, which are so much lower and smaller that they appear quite insignificant. Similarly, the immediate natural surroundings of the temple are unobtrusive and have no marked characteristics. The position of the northern and western stoas echoes the relationship between two low chains of hills that meet one another at a right angle, to north and west.

---

[1] Wilhelm Dörpfeld, "Der Tempel von Sunion," Deutsches Archäologisches Institut, *Mitteilungen Athenische Abteilung* 9, 1884, p. 331.
[2] Valerios Staïs, Τό Σούνιον καί οἱ ναοί Ποσειδῶνος καί Ἀθηνᾶς, p. 16.
[3] Dörpfeld, "Der Tempel von Sunion," p. 335.
[4] Ibid., p. 336.
[5] [The dating and sequence of the four temples attributed by most authorities to the same unknown "Hephaisteion architect" have long been a matter of dispute. W. B. Dinsmoor puts the Hephaisteion of Athens first: "all the evidence suggests 449 B.C. for the beginning of the work" (*Architecture of Ancient Greece*, London: Batsford, 1950, p. 180). In his opinion, "the temple at Sunium may have been designed about 444 B.C., that of Ares at Athens about 440 B.C., and that at Rhamnus in 436 B.C." (ibid., p. 182).]

Works Consulted by the Author
Dörpfeld, Wilhelm. "Der Tempel von Sunion." Deutsches Archäologisches Institut. *Mitteilungen. Athenische Abteilung* 9, 1884.

Fabricus, Ernst. "Die Skulpturen vom Tempel in Sounion." Ibid.

Orlandos, Anastasios K. "Τό ἀέτωμα τοῦ ἐν Σουνίω ναοῦ τοῦ Ποσειδῶνος." Ἀρχαιολογική Ἐφημερίς, 1915.

———. "Τοῦ ἐν Σουνίω ναοῦ τοῦ Ποσειδῶνος τοῖχοι καί ὀροφή." Ibid., 1917.

Staïs, Valerios, "Ἀνασκαφαί ἐν Σουνίω." Ibid., 1900.

———. "Σουνίου ἀνασκαφαί." Ibid., 1917.

———. Τό Σούνιον καί οἱ ναοί Ποσειδῶνος καί Ἀθηνᾶς. Athens: Library of the Archaeological Society, 1920.

Additional References
William H. Plommer. "Three Attic Temples," pt. 2, "The Temple of Poseidon." British School at Athens, *Annual* 45, 1950, pp. 78–94. (A detailed account of the measurements of the temple.)

———. "The Temple of Poseidon on Cape Sunium: Some Further Questions." *BSA* 55, 1960, pp. 218–233.

51 Sounion, Sacred Precinct of Poseidon. View
from point A, 1969.

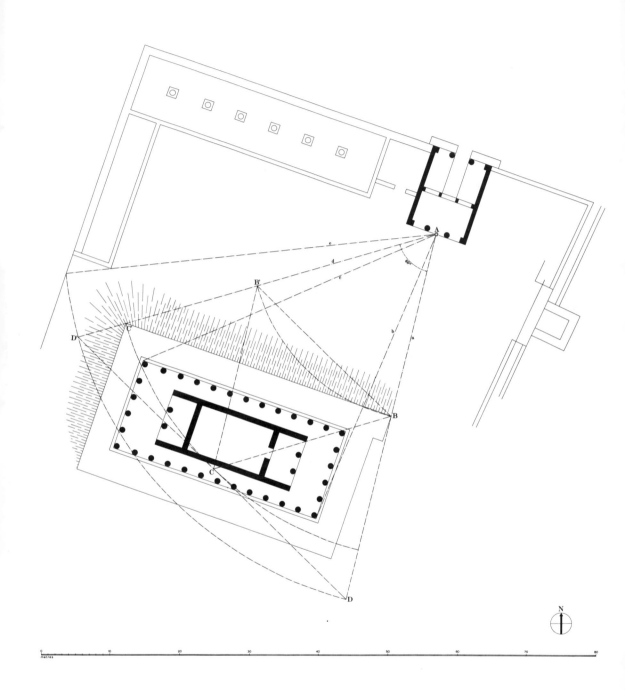

53 Sounion, Sacred Precinct of Poseidon.
General Plan. (Staïs.)

54 Sounion, Sacred Precinct of Poseidon.
View of temple. (Plommer.)

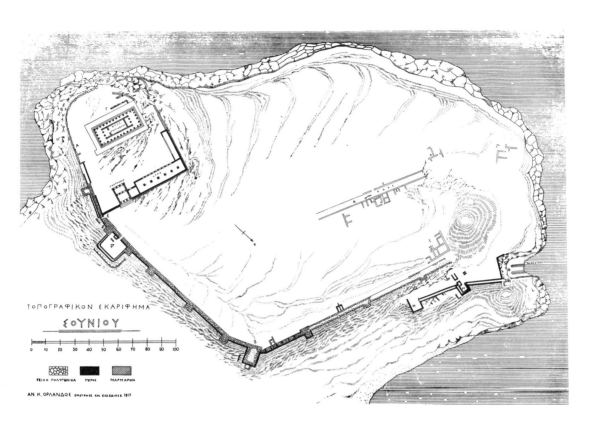

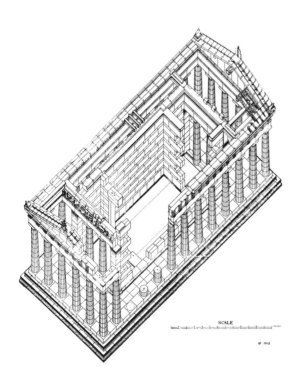

The Agora at Pergamon, Third Century B.C.

It is not known precisely when construction of the Pergamon agora began, but the existing ruins seem to indicate that the entire site dates from the same period—the era of the Seleucid kings.[1] It is thought that the western half of the agora and the stoas were built at the same time[2] and that the temple of Athena and the altar of Zeus were erected somewhat later.

Organization of the Site, Third or Second Century B.C. There were two entrances, north and south, at the points where an older road crossed the agora. They are marked A and B on the plan (Fig. 56). Through entrance A passed all the traffic proceeding from the high citadel to the lower city, south of the agora (Fig. 57). Similarly, entrance B was used by all traffic from the lower city proceeding to the citadel.

SIGHT LINES FROM POINT A

Point A is situated in the center of the entrance at the first spot from which the entire western agora can be seen.

a to farthest (southern) corner of the southeast stoa (C on the plan)

b to left corner of the central group of monuments (F on the plan)

c to right corner of the central group of monuments; left corner of the temple façade (D' on the plan)

d to left corner of the exedra; right (northeast) corner of the temple façade

e to middle corner of the exedra; right (northwest) corner of the temple (C' on the plan)

f to right corner of the exedra; left corner of the northwest building (D' on the plan)

g to a line parallel to the northern retaining wall

ANGLES OF VISION FROM POINT A

Angle $ab = 30° = 180°/6$.
Angle $bg = 60° = 180°/3$.

Thus, the northern boundary of the upper half of the agora is based on the position of line g.

DISTANCES FROM POINT A

AC, along line $a = AC'$ along line $e = 52.4$ m.

This is exactly 100 Egyptian ells;[3] i.e., $100 \times 0.524 = 52.4$ m.

AD' along line $c = AD''$ along line $f = 45.37$ m.

If an arc is described with center A and radius AD' to cut line b at D, then $AD' = AD = AC \sqrt{3}/2$, and so

$45.37 = 52.40 \times 1.732/2$.

Thus ACD is a right-angled triangle whose side $AC = 52.4$ m and angle $ab = 30°$.

FIELD OF VISION FROM POINT A

The composition of the layout is determined by the angles of 30° and 60° and the ratio resulting from them ($x : x \sqrt{3}/2$). In other words, there is a twelvefold division of the total area of 360°.

The field of vision is fully enclosed. The view of the temple façade between lines c and d is kept clear. Line AG, which points due west to the sunset, lies exactly between AE and AD' (line c).

SIGHT LINES FROM POINT B

At point B, in the center of the southern entrance to the site, the road is 3 m lower than the surface of the western half of the agora. Only when the spectator moves to point B' is his eye at the same height as the parapet, i.e., 0.70 m above ground level. B' is thus the first point from which a view of the site can be gained; it can therefore be considered a visual entrance to the site. If the road were not sunk, a view of the open area without buildings that lies south of the central group of monuments might be obtained between points B and B' (see Fig. 55). As it is, however, the layout of the site permits no open views, for point B' the view of the open area is already closed by the most southerly of the central group of monuments. This point also determines the line $B'E$.

(Notes to this page are on page 110.)

55   Pergamon, Agora. View from point A to the
west, 1936.

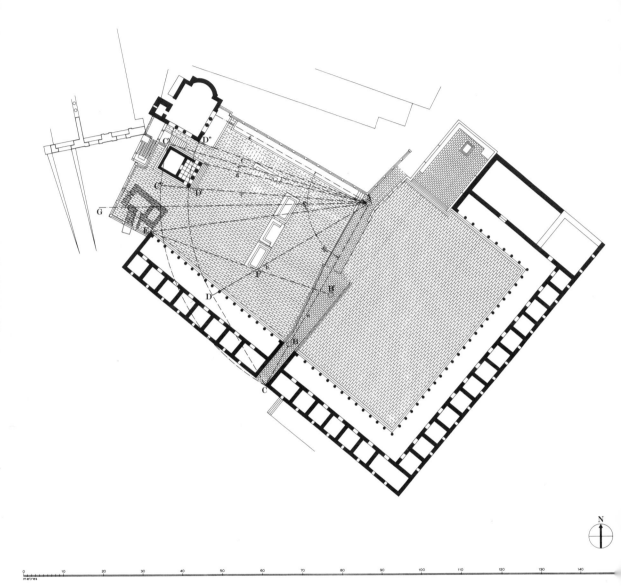

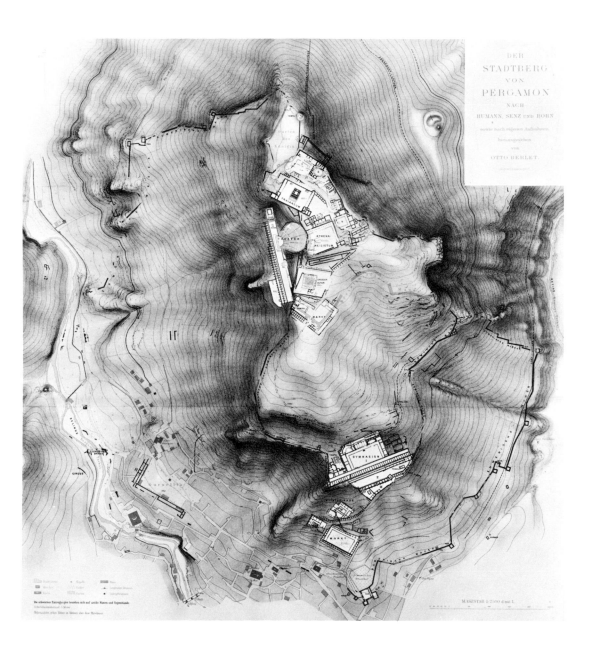

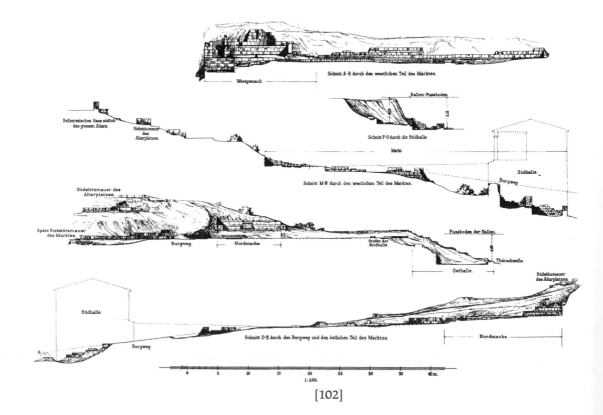

Schnitt A-B durch den westlichen Teil des Marktes.

Westgemach

Hallen-Fussboden

Schnitt F-G durch die Südhalle

Hellenistisches Haus südlich
des grossen Altars.

Südstützmauer
des
Altarplatzes.

Markt

Südhalle.

Schnitt M-N durch den westlichen Teil des Marktes.

Burgweg

Südstützmauer des
Altarplatzes.

Späte Nordstützmauer
des Marktes.

Fussboden der Hallen.

Burgweg.   Nordnische.

Stufen der
Nordhalle.

Thürschwelle.

Osthalle.

Südstützmauer
des Altarplatzes.

Südhalle

Burgweg

Schnitt D-E durch den Burgweg und den östlichen Teil des Marktes.

Nordnische.

0   5   10   15   20   25   30   35   40 m.
1:250.

59 Pergamon, Agora. General plan. (Schrammen.)

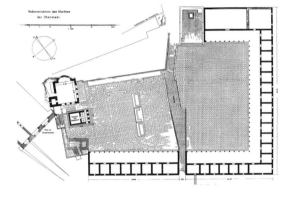

The Sacred Precinct of Athena at Pergamon, Second Century B.C.

Although the temple of Athena was built in the fourth century B.C., when Pergamon was only a small town, its precinct was not created until the reign of King Eumenes II (197–159 B.C.), at a time when many other urban changes were taking place. The existing temple served as the starting point for the layout of the precinct, which was formed by the erection of three stoas. The only remaining monument, which stands in the center of the precinct, dates from the Roman era. We can be fairly certain that it replaced a Hellenistic monument, since its position fits into the Hellenistic layout, and since we know that in the Hellenistic period the precinct was adorned with many famous statues, of which there are now no traces.

Organization of the Site, 197–159 B.C. The precinct had two entrances, a main entrance (A on the plan, Fig. 61) from the east through the propylon and a minor entrance (B on the plan) through the northern stoa.

SIGHT LINES FROM POINT A

(* indicates that the exact position of this structure is not certain.)

Point A lies on the platform of the propylon, at the crossing of its axis with the line of the top step of the eastern stoa.

a to right (northwest) corner of the southern stoa (D on the plan); left corner of the altar of Athena*

b to right corner of the altar of Athena*; pronounced angle in the boundary wall

c to left (southeast) corner of the temple of Athena (E' on the plan); another angle in the boundary wall

d to left tangent of the central monument; right corner of the temple of Athena (junction with boundary wall)

e to right tangent of the central monument; left (southeast) corner of the northern stoa F'' on the plan).

ANGLES OF VISION FROM POINT A

Angle $ce = 30° = 180°/6$.

The angle between line e and the top step of

the eastern stoa $= 60° = 180°/3$.

DISTANCES FROM POINT A

Point A to the northeast corner of the precinct (C'') = 37.0 m. If an arc is described from A with radius AC'', it touches the nearest point of the central monument at C' and cuts a line a at a point C.

The distance along line a from point A to the northwest corner of the southern stoa (D) = 55.5 m. An arc with radius AD touches the northeast corner of the temple (D').

The distance along line c from point A to the southeast corner of the temple (E') = 64.0 m.

The distance along line e from point A to the southeast corner of the northern stoa (F'') = 74.0 m. An arc with radius AF'' touches the southwest corner of the temple (F') and perhaps denotes the northeast corner of the altar of Athena* (F).

Hence $AC' = AC'' = 37.0 \text{ m} = 74.0 \text{ m}/2 = AF''/2$,

and $AD = AD' = 55.5 \text{ m} = 3AF''/4$,

or AC' = the small side of the right-angled triangle AF''C''.

Also $AD = AD' = 55.5 \text{ m} = 3AF''/4$, or AD = three-quarters of the large side of the triangle AF''C''.

In other words, the organization of the space is determined by the right-angled triangle AF''C'' and the use of the angle of 30°, or a twelvefold division of the total area of 360°.

FIELD OF VISION FROM POINT A

From left to right we can see (Fig. 60)

the southern stoa

the altar of Athena*

an open view, obstructed only by the low parapet of the enclosure wall

the temple of Athena

the circular central monument

the northern stoa.

The path to the altar and to the entrance of the temple of Athena is emphasized by an open view; line c, leading to point E' at the southeast

[104]

corner of the temple, lies directly perpendicular to the main entrance to the precinct through the propylon. The open field of vision is oriented 21° south of west.

The right-angled triangle $AF''C''$ is similar to the triangle formed by half the base of the temple, $E'D'G$, which also has angles of 30°, 60°, and 90°. The triangle $E'D'G$ lies so that its sides are either parallel or perpendicular to the sides of the triangle $AF''C''$. Thus, for example,

AF'' is parallel to GD'

AC'' is parallel to $E'G$

$E'D'$ is perpendicular to AF''.

As we have mentioned, the temple was built two centuries before the precinct was laid out, and we may conclude that its position and proportions determined the form, size, and orientation of the Hellenistic stoas.

SIGHT LINES FROM POINT B

This small entrance gave access to the sacred precinct from the north. Point B lies on the edge of the top step in the center of the opening.

h to left tangent of the central monument; southeast corner of the precinct

g to left (northeast) corner of the temple of Athena (D' on the plan), right (northwest) corner of the southern stoa (D on the plan)

f to right (northwest) corner of the temple (G on the plan); and angle in the boundary wall.

(See page 110 for list of works consulted.)

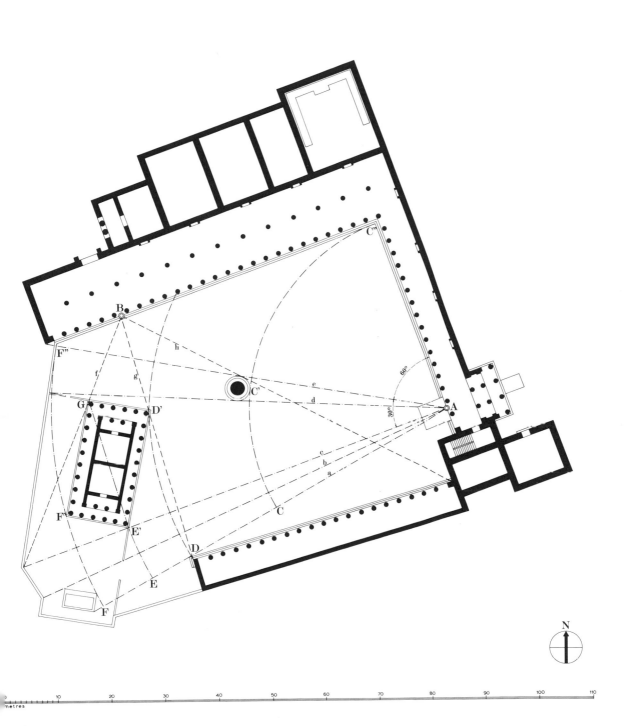

62 Pergamon, Sacred Precinct of Athena. Plan.
(Bohn.)

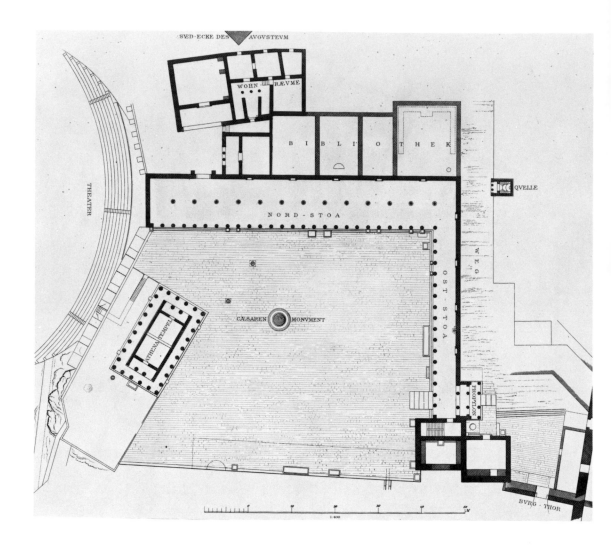

63 Pergamon, Sacred Precinct of Athena. Reconstruction, seen from the south. (Bohn.)

The Altar of Zeus at Pergamon, Second Century B.C.

Neither the exact date of the great altar of Zeus nor the outlines of its terrace are precisely known, but it is generally believed that it was built at the time of King Eumenes II (197–159 B.C.). This assumption is based on the style of the sculptures and on the inscriptions that adorn it, as well as on its enormous dimensions. The outbreak of hostilities following Eumenes' reign also make it unlikely that a monument of this size could have been undertaken much later than this date. We have thus accepted this date.

Organization of the Site. Three entrances seem likely, although they have not been definitely proved (Fig. 64). There is slight evidence of a propylon on the east boundary, and point *A* has been established as its center. From this point, the altar appears within an angle of 60°. In the northwest corner of the terrace, there are signs of some steps leading down from an upper terrace, although their beginning and end have not been ascertained. If we assume that an entrance was situated at the foot of the steps, and establish point *B* as its center, we find that the altar again appears within an angle of 60° and, further, that the west side of the altar lies directly perpendicular to point *B*. A third entrance (point *C*) is assumed to lie at the head of a flight of steps—of which some traces have also been found—leading down to a lower terrace to the south.

We find that the sight lines from each of these three entrances (assuming that their positions have been accurately determined) coincide, that each encompasses two corners of the altar, and that together they form a single equilateral triangle *ABC*, within which the rectangle of the altar is precisely placed. We also find that from entrance *A* there is a view due west across the altar to the only visible peak of a mountain range lying on the far side of the valley of a tributary of the Caicus. The position of the altar thus acknowledges and emphasizes the dominating feature of the landscape (see Fig. 57).

[1] Jakob Schrammen, *Der grosse Altar; der obere Markt,* Berlin, Staatliche Museen, Die Altertümer von Pergamon, vol. 3, pt. 1, pp. 93, 118.
[2] Ibid., p. 106.
[3] Hans Schleif told me that one should not be confused by the use of the term "Egyptian ells." The ell used at Pergamon was developed there, and it is a matter of chance that it was identical with the Egyptian royal ell. [See also Chapter 3, note 4.]

Works Consulted by the Author
Bohn, Richard. *Das Heiligtum der Athena Polias Nikephoros.* Berlin, Staatliche Museen. Die Altertümer von Pergamon, vol. 2. Berlin: Spemann, 1885.

Conze, Alexander, et al. *Stadt und Landschaft.* Berlin, Staatliche Museen. Die Altertümer von Pergamon, vol. 1. Berlin: Reimer, 1913.

Schrammen, Jakob. *Der grosse Altar; der obere Markt.* Berlin, Staatliche Museen. Die Altertümer von Pergamon, vol. 3, pt. 1. Berlin: Reimer, 1906.

Additional References
Humann, Carl. *Der Pergamon Altar.* Dortmund: Ardey, 1959.

Rohde, Elisabeth. *Pergamon.* Berlin: Henschel, 1961.
Schober, Arnold. *Die Kunst von Pergamon.* Vienna: Rohrer, 1951.

Zschietzschmann, Willy. "Pergamon." In Pauly, A. F. von, ed. *Real-Encyclopädie der classischen Altertumswissenschaft.* Stuttgart: Metzler, 1937. XIX, pp. 1235–1264.

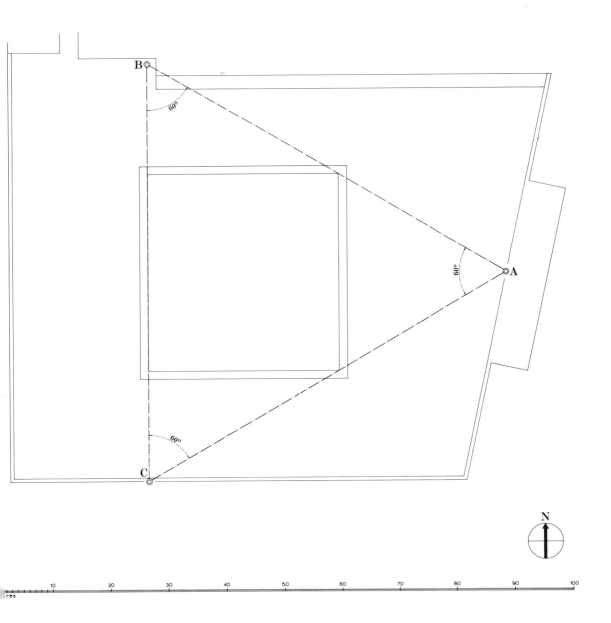

65   Pergamon, Altar of Zeus and Agora. Plan.
(Schrammen.)

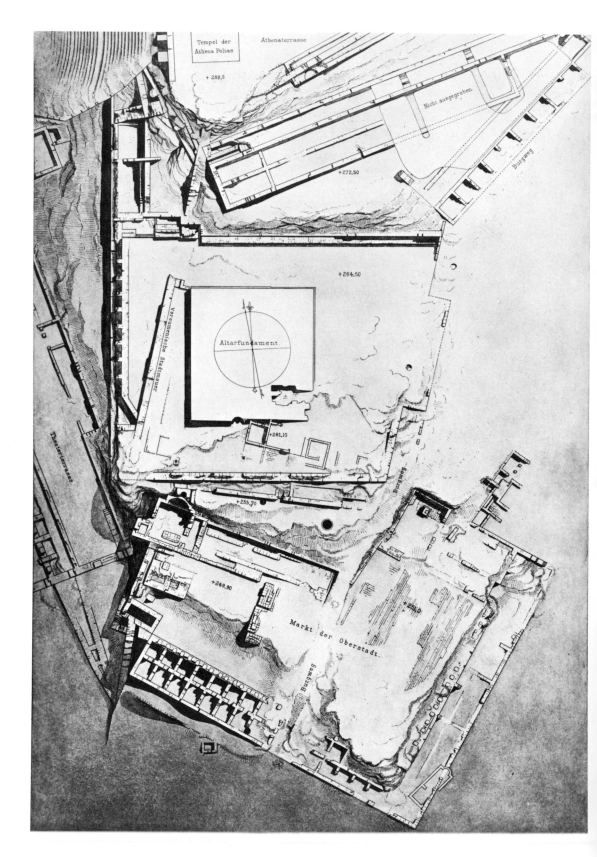

66 Pergamon, Altar of Zeus. Reconstruction.
(Schrammen.)

6 Use of the Ten-Part System

The Heraion at Samos, Sixth Century B.C.

As a result of the work of archaeologists such as Theodor Wiegand, Martin Schede, Ernst Buschor, and Hans Schleif, we have a clear picture of the development of this site from the early archaic period to early Christian times.

The great temple was built and rebuilt before the sixth century B.C. To the east of the temple lay the great altar of Hera, which was rebuilt seven times at seven different periods. In the late seventh century there were also several treasuries, a stoa, and some other buildings. Figure 68 is based on Schleif's reconstruction of the site during this period.

About 550 B.C., the architects Rhoikos and Theodoros demolished nearly all the earlier buildings and erected the first great temple of Hera with its accompanying great altar (Fig. 70). A small building (G on the plan) also dates from this period.

Only a few years later, this temple was burned down, and the Samians, probably still under the rule of Polykrates, planned and began construction of another great temple, although it was never fully completed. As long as this great temple of Hera remained in use, the appearance of the forecourt remained unchanged, except that more votive offerings accumulated around it.[2] Figure 71 shows the site as it was from the fifth to the second century B.C.

By the Augustan era the temple had lost its significance and was used as a storehouse for votive offerings. Gradually, the site became completely altered through the erection of many small buildings, until by the early Christian period it was a mass of small structures. Figure 74 shows the area surrounding the great altar in the first century A.D.[3]

I divided the development of the site into four phases:

1

The period just before the Rhoikos temple (Fig. 68). I have assumed this to be representative of the layout throughout the early periods, as there seems to have been only a slight difference between them.

2

The Rhoikos period, mid-sixth century B.C. (Fig. 70).

3

The period of the new great temple, from the end of the sixth century B.C. until the second century B.C. (Fig. 71).

4

The early Roman period, first century A.D. (Fig. 74).

No entrance has been definitely established on the site at any of these four periods. It seems that for a short time only the building southeast of the temple served as a propylon, but this was demolished before the great altar was built over it in the time of Rhoikos. It therefore cannot be considered as acting as an entrance in later periods. In endeavoring to discover from the important sightlines where an entrance might have been, I was obliged to concentrate upon the third and fourth periods, as too few buildings remained from the earlier periods to allow a test of the system to be made. As a result of my calculations, I found that it was possible to establish a point A between the two side walls (antae) of a small building, not fully excavated and thus not fully described, which, according to a verbal statement by Hans Schleif, might well have been a propylon. I have therefore postulated that a propylon or at least an entrance existed on this site, and I have investigated all four site plans to determine whether or not an entrance could have existed at this point.[4]

Heraion I, Early Sixth Century

Organization of the Site. This is the period of temple II, altar VII, and the southern temenos (the great southwestern building). The layout had evolved gradually from the geometric period until the sixth century (Fig. 68). Although our supposition that point A represents the entrance is not contradicted by any features of the layout, on the other hand, there is no strong evidence to support it, since no explicit use is made of specific angles and distances.

If we take the southeast building to represent the propylon at this time, as do the excavators, we find that no aspects of the system apply. We must therefore conclude that this was not the entrance, or that the system was not known in Samos, or that this entrance, which was the last building to be erected, could not be placed in accordance with the system.

Heraion II, Mid-Sixth Century B.C.

Organization of the Site. Point A lies in the center of the edge of the top step of building I, assumed to be the propylon (Fig. 69).

SIGHT LINES FROM POINT A

a to right corner of the small building to the east; left (northeast) corner of the great altar

b to left (northeast) corner of the temple of Hera; right (southwest) corner of the great altar (B on the plan)

c to right (northwest) corner of the temple of Hera

c' to extension of line c to the east.

ANGLES OF VISION FROM POINT A

Angle $c'a = 36° = 180°/5$.

Angle $ab = 36° = 180°/5$.

Angle $bc = 108° = 3 \times 180°/5$.

DISTANCES FROM POINT A

The distance from point A along line b to the southwest corner of the great altar (B on plan) $= 69.80$ m.

The distance from point A to the nearest (northwest) corner of the great altar (C on the plan) $= 43.13$ m.

Hence $AC/AB = 43.13/69.80 = 0.618/1 = (\sqrt{5} - 1)/2$ or the golden section.

Also, $AB = 69.80 = 200 \times 0.349$ or 200 Ionic feet.[5]

FIELD OF VISION FROM POINT A

The hypothesis that point A represents an

entrance, planned at the same time as the Rhoikos layout of the site, is supported by the following factors:

1
the angles within which the main buildings of the site are seen from point A are $180°/5$, $180°/5$, $3 \times 180°/5$;

2
the relation of the distances from point A to the great altar (i.e., the golden section) and their unit of measure (i.e., the Ionic foot);

3
the prolongation of line c eastward lies along the front line of the assumed propylon, thus perpendicular to its axis.

Heraion III, End of the Sixth Century B.C.

Organization of the Site. The layout was altered by several new constructions: the great new temple, a small structure surrounded by a single row of columns (the monopteros), and a row of votive offerings, which were being erected when the great temple was being built.

The assumed entrance has been maintained at point A.

SIGHT LINES FROM POINT A

a to right corner of the small building to the east (G on the plan) left (northeast) corner of the great altar (F on the plan)

b to right (southwest) corner of the great altar (B on the plan)

d to left (southeast) corner of the "monopteros" (F'' on the plan); right (western) end of the row of votive offerings (D'' on the plan)

e to right (northwest) corner of the "monopteros"; left (southeast) corner of the great temple (D on the plan).

ANGLES OF VISION FROM POINT A

Angle ab remains the same $= 36° = 180°/5$.

Angle $bd = 37° = $ ca. $36° = 180°/5$.

DISTANCES FROM POINT A

The distance from point A along line e to point D' at the southeast corner of the temple $= 78.50$ m.

If we describe an arc with radius AD, we find it touches the western end of the row of votive offerings (D'' on the plan) and the southeast corner of the great altar (D on the plan).

According to measurements taken on the plans, $AD' = 78.50$ m; $AD'' = 78.50$ m; $AD = 78.00$ m.

The distance from point A along line a to point F at the northeast corner of the great altar $= 56.00$ m.

If we describe an arc with radius AF, we find it approximately meets the southeast corner of the monopteros at F' along line d. According to measurements taken on the plans, $AF' = 57.00$ m.

FIELD OF VISION FROM POINT A

From point A the monopteros is linked optically with the temple.

Although line cc' now meets the temple at the corner of its second row of columns, our assumption that point A represents the entrance is not necessarily invalidated, since the perpendicular of the temple exactly bisects the angle bd, and the line of votive offerings starting from point D'' runs parallel to cc'. It may be added, without attaching much importance to the observation, that the temple's northern line of columns was never actually built.

Heraion IV, First Century A.D.

Organization of the Site. Considerable changes were made in the early Roman period. As has already been noted at other sites, the Romans ignored the earlier organization of the layout and concentrated on the use of the right-angled triangle.

The site now contains a wide central pathway (attested by a broad strip of land devoid of buildings, with a water channel running through its center) and short paths that meet it at right angles. This new Roman route starts from point A, which we have taken to represent the entrance in earlier periods. That point A now marks the start of an important north-

south axis greatly strengthens our case, especially since the route runs parallel to the façades of several existing structures such as the temple and the altar. The organization of the site is no longer based on lines of sight, angles of vision, or relations between distances but is entirely determined by right-angled axes.

---

[1] I have studied this site only from the plans and reports prepared by the excavators.
[2] Hans Schleif, "Heraion von Samos: Das Vorgelände des Tempels," *Deutsches Archäologisches Institut, Mitteilungen, Athenische Abteilung* 58, 1933, p. 217.
[3] For its further development see Schleif's four articles "Heraion von Samos," *AthMitt.* 58, 1933.
[4] [According to Buschor and Ziegenaus ("Heraion 1959," p. 2), at the time of the Rhoikos temple there were four sacred ways, though probably still without formal entrance structures. Two appeared to come from the direction of the town to the east, a third from the sea to the south, and a fourth from the north. These sacred ways are shown in a map in the short account of the sequence of excavations at Samos by Hans Walter, *Das griechische Heiligtum,* 1965, and the building assumed by Doxiadis to have been a propylon is there shown to have been built at the time of Polykrates (538–522 B.C.), although no mention is made of its use (see Doxiadis' Figs. 72, 75). According to Oscar Ziegenaus ("Die Tempelgruppe im Norden des Altarplatzes," 1957, p. 125), "This building is much larger than one would expect a treasury to be at this period, and although the form of its plan is reminiscent of a propylon, its position in the sacred precinct—far from the archaic boundary of the temenos—makes this impossible." Ziegenaus points out that the structure has not yet been fully excavated and that a final verdict must await a restudy of this part of the precinct.]
[5] [For discussion of ancient Greek feet see Chapter 3, note 4.]

Works Consulted by the Author

Buschor, Ernst. "Heraion von Samos: frühe Bauten." Deutsches Archäologisches Institut. *Mitteilungen. Athenische Abteilung* 55, 1930, pp. 1–99.

———, and Schleif, Hans. "Heraion von Samos: der Altarplatz der Frühzeit." *AthMitt.* 55, 1930, pp. 146–173.

Schede, Martin. "Zweiter vorläufiger Bericht über die Ausgrabungen auf Samos." Preussische Akademie der Wissenschaften. *Abhandlungen. Philosophische-Historische Klasse,* 1929, no. 3, pp. 1–26.

Schleif, Hans. "Der grosse Altar der Hera von Samos." *AthMitt.* 58, 1933, pp. 174–210.

Schleif, Hans. "Heraion von Samos: das Vorgelände des Tempels." *AthMitt.* 58, 1933, pp. 211–247.

Wiegand, Theodor. "Erster vorläufiger Bericht über die Ausgrabungen in Samos." *AbhPreuss.,* 1911, no. 5, pp. 1–24.

Additional References

Buschor, Ernst. "Imbraso." Deutsches Archäologisches Institut. *Mitteilungen. Athenische Abteilung* 68, 1953, pp. 1-10.

————, and Ziegenaus, Oscar. "Heraion 1959." *AthMitt.* 72, 1957, pp. 52-64.

Johannes, Heinz. "Die Säulenbasen vom Heratempel des Rhoikos." *AthMitt.* 62, 1937, pp. 13-37.

Ohly, Dieter. "Die Göttin und ihre Basis." *AthMitt.* 68, 1953, pp. 25-50.

Reuther, Oscar. *Der Heratempel von Samos: der Bau seit der Zeit des Polykrates.* Berlin: Mann, 1957.

Walter, Hans. *Das griechische Heiligtum: Heraion von Samos.* Munich: Piper, 1965.

Wrede, Walther. "Vorgeschichtliches in der Stadt Samos: Fundtatsachen." *AthMitt.* 60-61, 1935-1936, pp. 112-124.

Ziegenaus, Oscar. "Der Südbau: Ergänzende Untersuchungen." *AthMitt.* 72, 1957, pp. 65-76.

————. "Die Tempelgruppe im Norden des Altarplatzes." *AthMitt.* 72, 1957, pp. 87-151.

67   Samos, Heraion. View from point A, 1969. The man at the left is standing at the northeast corner of the great altar. In the foreground are many votive offerings. The man in the center (left of the single column) is at the northwest corner of the monopteros, and directly behind him is the southwest corner of the great temple. The column is the northernmost of the four facing the steps.

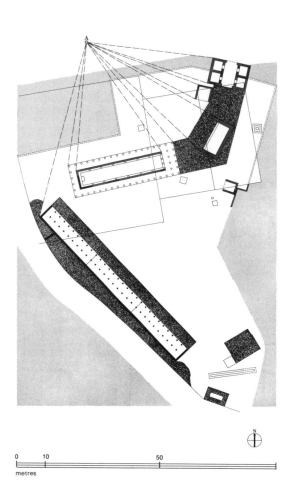

70   Samos, Heraion II, Rhoikos period. Plan.

71   Samos, Heraion III, Classical period. Plan.

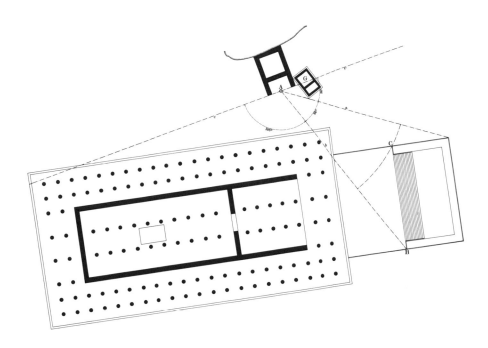

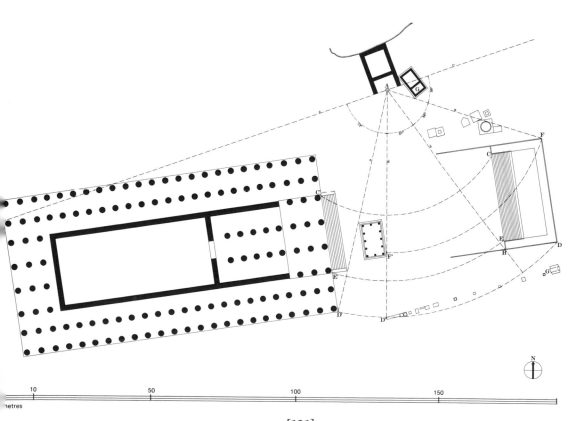

N

10   50   100   150

metres

[121]

72   Samos, Heraion III, Classical period. Plan.
(Walter.)

73   Samos, Heraion. Reconstruction of the great
altar. (Walter.)

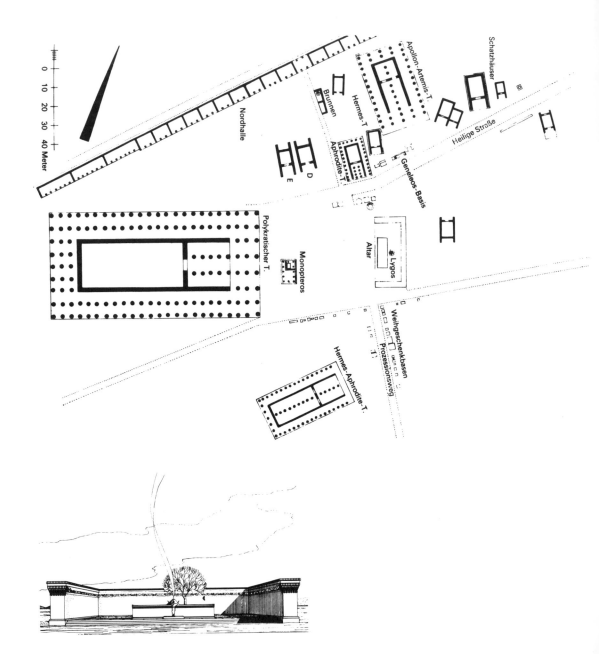

74   Samos, Heraion IV, Roman period. Plan.

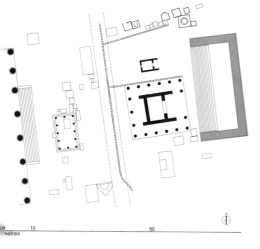

10   50
metres

75 Samos, Heraion. General plan showing four
different periods. (Walter.)

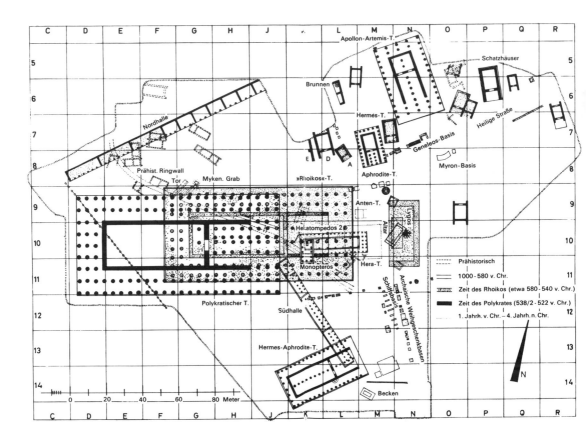

The Asclepeion at Cos,
Fourth, Third, and Second Centuries B.C.

This site bears evidence of building activity at several different periods.[1] Although the only remains extant from before the third century B.C. are those of the first altar, built between 350 and 330 B.C., there is ample evidence of extensive construction during the first golden age of the island of Cos, between 300 and 205 B.C.,[2] and in later centuries.

Structures dating from the first active period include the lower terrace (terrace I) with its stoas and chambers (300–250 B.C.) and the earliest buildings on the middle terrace (terrace II), such as building E in Figure 77 and the buildings shown as C and D. Temple B and the exedra on terrace II were built a little later, the former dating probably from about 280 B.C.

It seems likely that the magnificent development of the site was begun soon after 190 B.C. following the island's great victories in 197 and 190 B.C., although evidence from the structures shows that the project was not completed until about 160 or 150 B.C.[3]

The late Hellenistic altar on the middle terrace (K on the plan) was built later than temple B and the exedra, between 160 and 150 B.C. Temple C and building D were built in Roman times, the former dating from late in the Antonine period (the second half of the second century B.C.)

Asclepeion, Lower Terrace (Terrace I), 300–250 B.C.

Organization of the Site. This northern and lowest terrace has a central entrance from the north. Point F lies midway between two columns of the stoa on the axis of the outer stairway.

SIGHT LINES FROM POINT F

a to right (southwest) corner of the eastern stoa on terrace I

b to left (northeast) corner of temple C on terrace II

c to right corner of the exedra on terrace II

d to right corner of the steps leading up to terrace II; middle corner (northeast) of temple B on terrace II

e to right (northwest) corner of temple B on terrace II; right (northwest) corner of the western stoa on terrace III

f to left (southeast) corner of the western stoa on terrace I.

ANGLES OF VISION FROM POINT F

Angle $ab = 34° = $ ca. $36° = 180°/5$.

Angle $bd = 36° = 180°/5$.

Angle $df = 36° = 180°/5$.

Hence angle $af = 34° + 36° + 36° = 106° = $ ca. $108° = 3 \times 180°/5$.

DISTANCES FROM POINT F

The distance from F to either end of the northern stoa (G and G'' on the plan) $= 47.50$ m. If a semicircle is described with radius FG, it touches the supporting wall of terrace II at point G'. The ground plan of terrace I thus has a ratio of $1:2$, although it is not a mathematical rectangle.

Asclepeion, Middle Terrace (Terrace II), Second Century B.C.

Organization of the Site. Although the middle terrace had three distinct forms in three consecutive periods, I have been obliged to base my investigations on the form of the last period, as there was not sufficiently precise information concerning the earlier ones.

From 300 to 250 B.C. the terrace contained the first altar (K on the plan, Fig. 77), building E, earlier buildings below C and D, temple B, and the exedra. It is not possible to show whether or not these were disposed according to a prearranged plan.

From about 150 B.C. until the first century A.D. the terrace contained the later altar, all the former buildings, and the steps leading to the upper terrace (terrace III).

At the end of the second century A.D. building E, temple B, the exedra, and the later altar (K on the plan) remained from earlier periods, and temple C and building D were added.

It can be recognized that the main entrance would lie on the axis at the head of the central flight of steps leading up from the lower terrace (terrace I), but, as the upper part of these steps are missing, I have had to assume a probable location for this point: H on the plan.

SIGHT LINES FROM POINT H

g to left (northeast) corner of the building group E on the plan

h to right (southwest) corner of building E; left (northeast) corner of temple C

i to left (northeast) corner of the altar (K on the plan); right (southwest) corner of temple C; left corner of the exedra

j to left (northeast) corner of temple A on terrace III

k to left (southeast) corner of temple B on terrace II

l to right (northwest) corner of temple B on terrace II.

ANGLES OF VISION FROM POINT H

Angle $lk = 36° = 180°/5$.

Angle $kj = 36° = 180°/5$.

Angle $jg = 72° = 4 \times 180°/10$.

The entire layout as seen from point H thus falls within an angle of $144° = 36° + 36° + 72° = 4 \times 180°/5$.

DISTANCES FROM POINT H

The distance from H along line i to the northeast corner of the altar (K on the plan) = 10.50 m.

The distance from H to the nearest (northeast) corner of temple B (L' on the plan) = 17.00 m.

If an arc is described with radius HL', it touches the nearest (northwest) corner of temple C at L''.

It is found that $HK/HL = 10.5/17 = 0.618/1$ = golden section.

Asclepeion, Upper Terrace (Terrace III), circa 160 B.C.

Organization of the Site. It is known that the upper terrace was created between 160 and 150 B.C. The entrance was clearly on the steps leading from terrace II; its exact position has not been definitely established, but it must have lain on the axis of the steps and the temple, approximately at point I.

SIGHT LINES FROM POINT I

n to left (northeast) corner of the temple; left inner corner of the upper terrace (N' on the plan, Fig. 82)

o to right (northwest) corner of the temple; right inner corner of the upper terrace (N'' on the plan).

ANGLES OF VISION FROM POINT I

The angle between line n and the axis of the temple (IM) = $36° = 180°/5$.

The angle between line o and the axis of the temple (IM) = $36° = 180°/5$.

DISTANCES FROM POINT I

The distances from point I along lines n and o to point N' and N'' equal 69.80 m.

The distance from point I along the axis of the temple to its far end (M on the plan) = 43.13 m.

Hence $IM/IN = 43.13/69.80 = 0.618/1 =$ golden section.

The basic unit of the length of 69.80 m is the Ionian foot of 34.9 cm.

Hence $IN = 69.80$ m $= 200 \times 34.9$ cm $= 200$ Ionian feet.[5]

Further, if the triangle IMM' is turned on its side IM', we find that point M''' of the new triangle $IM'M'''$ determines the inner line of the eastern stoa. The inner line of the western stoa can be determined in the same way. The entire upper terrace is thus based on the 36° angle (180°/5) or on the ratio resulting from it, the golden section.

---

[1] My investigations were based on the official account of the German excavations, *Kos: Ergebnisse der deutschen Ausgrabungen und Forschungen,* edited by Rudolf Herzog. I did not examine the site.

[2] Paul Schazmann, "Die bauliche Entwicklung des Asklepieions," p. 72.

[3] Ibid.

[4] [Although these steps have since been restored, it is not certain that the restoration is correct.]

[5] [For discussion of ancient Greek feet see Chapter 3, note 4.]

Works Consulted by the Author
Herzog, Rudolf, ed. *Kos: Ergebnisse der deutschen Ausgrabungen und Forschungen,* vol. I. Berlin: Keller, 1932; in particular, Paul Schazmann, "Die bauliche Entwicklung des Asklepieions."

76 Cos, Asclepeion. View from point F, 1969. The
man at the left stands at the southwest corner of the
eastern stoa on terrace I. The columns of temple C
on terrace II can be seen to the right.

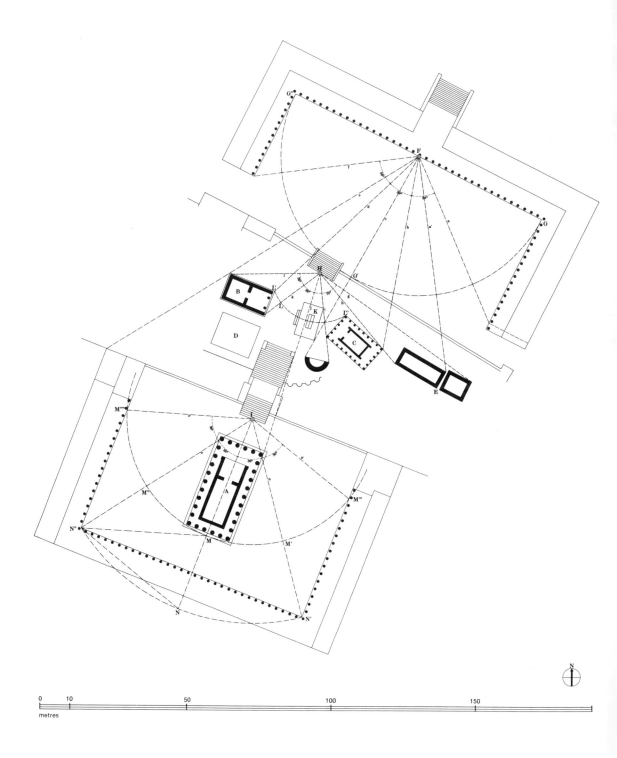

0   10   50   100   150

metres

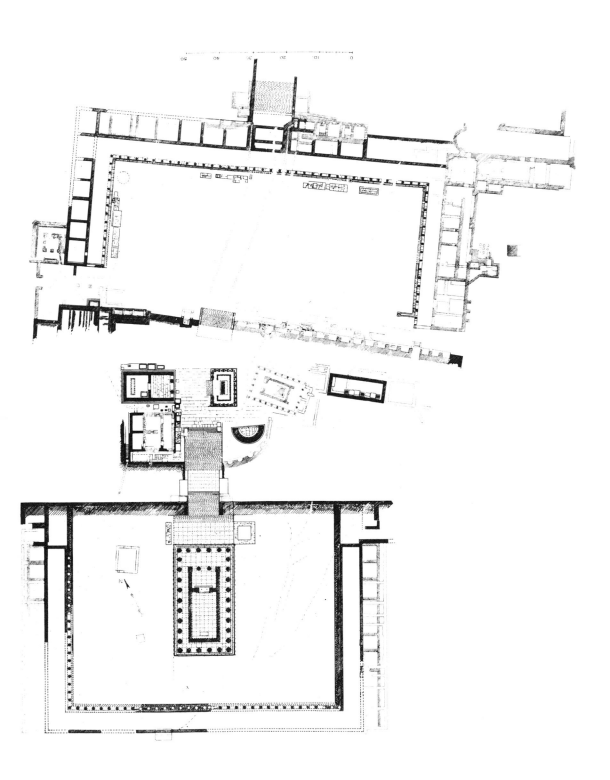

79 Cos, Asclepeion. Perspective of upper terrace from entrance. (Herzog.)

80 Cos, Asclepeion, Hellenistic period. Perspective from northeast. (Herzog.)

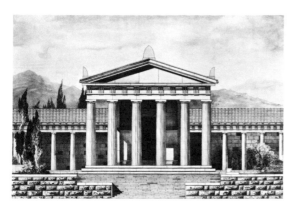

81a Cos, Asclepeion. View of the site in relation
to the sea, circa 1930. (Herzog.)

81b Cos, Asclepeion. View from upper terrace III looking north, 1969. The distant hill across the water directly fronts the flight of steps.

82 Cos, Asclepeion. View from point I, 1969. The
left corner of the temple is in line with the distant
corner of the upper terrace.

The Agora and the Temple of Athena at Priene, Fourth Century B.C.

The position from which I studied the layout of the site is to the west of the altar in the center of the agora at Priene. From this point, the temple of Athena appears exactly between two sight lines, *a* and *b* (Figs. 84, 86), that just touch the corners of the western and northern stoas and form an angle of 17° (18° = 180°/10). The temple stands on a higher level and, seen from here, forms a link between the ridge of the steep rocks to the right and the low buildings to the left (Fig. 85).

Although the entire agora was not built at the same time as the temple of Athena, "it is obvious that the agora was planned for in the layout of the city, which goes back to the fourth century B.C., and the leveling operations and retaining walls may well date back to that period, as well perhaps as the south stoa . . . and parts of the west and east stoas."[1] The temple of Athena was built in 344 B.C. Shortly after 150 B.C. a new stoa was built on the upper level, just south of the temple, *H* in Figure 84, shutting off the view of the temple from the central altar in the agora.

The great altar of Athena was erected to the east of the temple in 150 B.C., just to the right of sight line *b* (Fig. 84), perhaps to avoid blocking the view of the temple from the agora. Yet this choice of site would have been meaningless if (as indicated in Fig. 85) the terrace to the south of the temple, with its retaining wall, were at the same level as the floor of the later stoa, for then the great altar would be completely concealed from view. This means that, if sight line *b* were in fact taken into consideration, either the level of the original southern terrace was much lower, or its retaining wall was gradually stepped back, so that the altar could be visible from the agora.[2] As the propylon to the sacred precinct of Athena was built much later than the southern stoa, it is of no interest to this investigation.

The northern stoa on the agora, which is of importance to this study, was not built until 150 B.C., but it replaced a former shorter stoa, equal in length to the parallel southern stoa, which extended from the steps leading up to the temple of Athena to the steep path leading up to the theater.[3] The colonnade of this earlier stoa may lie below the Ionic columns of its successor, but it seems more likely that both had the same depth. Since the space of the earlier stoa was divided into two,[4] it was perhaps similar to the central part of the southern stoa. In this case the southwestern corner of the earlier stoa would have coincided with the same corner of the later one. This appears to be self-evident, as from the very first there must have been a desire to achieve a view of the temple of Athena framed by sight lines *a* and *b*. It is impossible to believe that this occurred as a happy accident after the erection of the temple and the western stoa.

If these observations are correct, they explain why there was a gateway at the eastern entrance to the agora but not at the western entry: the latter was left open so that there would be no obstruction to the view of the temple.

(Notes to this page are on page 146.)

[136]

83 Priene. General view from the west, circa 1898.
(Wiegand and Schrader.)

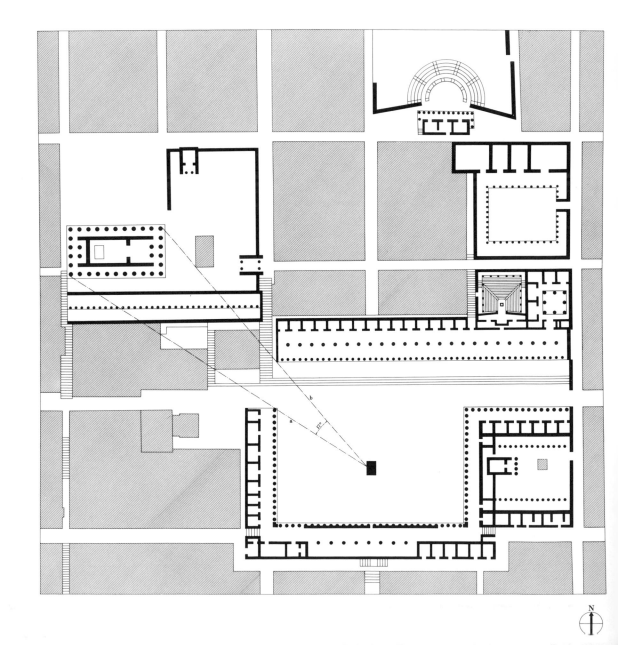

85   Priene, Temple of Athena. Perspective, from
the agora.

86 Priene, General plan.
(Wiegand and Schrader.)

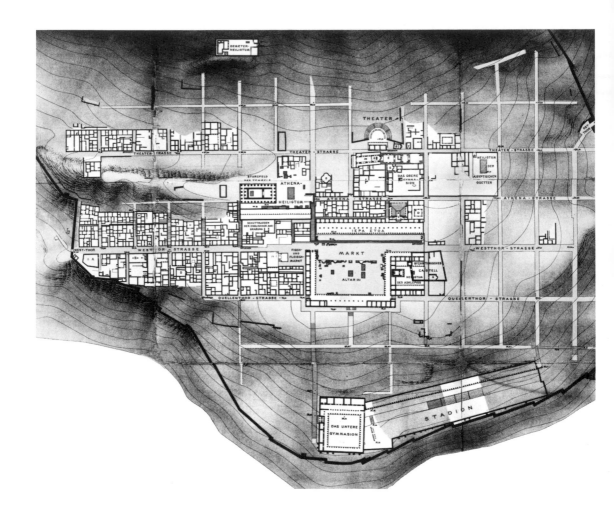

87   Priene, Sacred Precinct of Athena. Plan.
(Schede.)

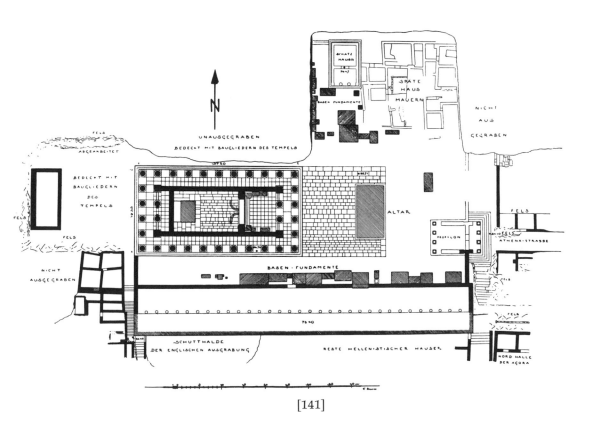

88   Priene, Agora. Section from north to south. (Wiegand and Schrader.)

89   Priene, Sacred Precinct of Athena. Perspective of southwest corner of the temple from the agora. (Schede.)

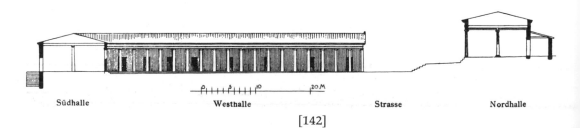

Südhalle   Westhalle   Strasse   Nordhalle

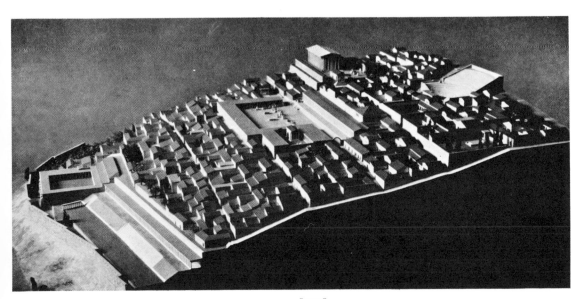

91   Priene. View of the site from the north, circa
1898. (Wiegand and Schrader.)

92   Priene, Agora. View from the east, circa 1898.
(Wiegand and Schrader.)

The Sacred Precinct of the Olympian Zeus at Priene, Third Century B.C.

This entire precinct was built to the east of the agora during the third century B.C. as a single project. The site has not been fully investigated, as a Byzantine fort was built over one of its corners, but the published plans permit us to make certain observations. Wiegand had attributed the temple to Asclepios, but Schede found that it was built to honor the Olympian Zeus.[5]

Organization of the Site. Entry was only through a gateway on the east. Point A lies in the center of this opening (Fig. 93).

SIGHT LINES FROM POINT A

a to left corner of the great altar; left (southwest) corner of the precinct (B on the plan)

b to left (southeast) corner of the temple

c to right (northeast) corner of the temple; perhaps the whole northern side of the temple

d to left corner of the pedestal (S on the plan); right (northwest) corner of the precinct.

ANGLES OF VISION FROM POINT A

Angle $bc = 18° = 180°/10$.
Angle $ad = 36° = 180°/5$.

The elevation of the temple as seen from point A thus occupies half the angle of vision of the entire precinct, although it is not placed symmetrically in the center of its western side.

DISTANCES FROM POINT A

The distance from point A along line a to point B on the plan $= 35.40$ m $= x$.

The distance from point A along line c to the façade of the temple (right corner of the upper step) $= 21.90$ m $= y$.

The distance from A to the northwest corner of the great altar $= 13.40$ m $= z$.

From this we see that

$x/y = 35.40/21.90 \times 1/0.618 =$ golden section;

$y/z = 21.90/13.40 = 1/0.612 = 1/0.618 =$ golden section.

The greatest distance AB, which measures 35.40 m, may also equal 100 Ionian feet, since the accepted measurement ($0.349 \times 100 =$

34.90 m) tended to vary slightly from place to place.[6]

FIELD OF VISION FROM POINT A

The observer is presented with a completely enclosed view, dominated by the angles of $18° = 180°/10$ and $36 = 180°/5$ and the proportion of the golden section which derives from them. In other words, this is a space determined by the tenfold division of the total field of $360°$.

---

[1] Theodor Wiegand and Hans Schrader, eds., *Priene*, p. 214.
[2] Ibid., p. 129.
[3] Ibid., p. 214.
[4] Ibid.
[5] Martin Schede, *Die Ruinen von Priene*, Berlin: De Gruyter, 1934, pp. 52–59.
[6] [For discussion of ancient Greek feet see Chapter 3, note 4.]

Works Consulted by the Author
Schede, Martin. Die Ruinen von Priene. Berlin: De Gruyter, 1934.

Wiegand, Theodor, and Schrader, Hans, eds. *Priene: Ergebnisse der Ausgrabungen und Untersuchungen in den Jahren 1896–1898.* Berlin: Reimer, 1904.

Additional References
Meyer, Bruno. "Das Propylon des sogenannten Asklepieions in Priene." Deutsches Archäologisches Institut. *Jahrbuch 49*, 1934.

Schede, Martin. *Die Ruinen von Priene.* 2nd ed. Berlin: De Gruyter, 1964.

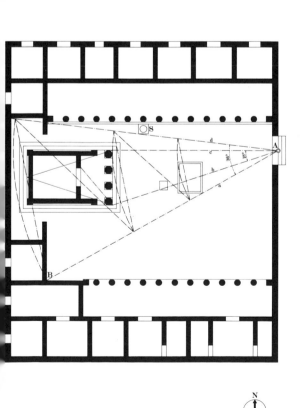

The Sacred Precinct of Artemis at Magnesia, Second Century B.C.

A sacred precinct of Artemis Leukophrene existed on this site from very early times, but the first building we know of was an archaic limestone temple that endured until the second century B.C. The precinct acquired its final form at the time of the rebuilding of the city in 400 B.C. At the end of the second century B.C., the famous architect Hermogenes constructed a new temple of Artemis, in which he incorporated for the first time his new architectural concepts. The altar of Artemis, in front of the temple, can also be attributed to Hermogenes.[1] Although the other structures cannot be dated accurately, it can be accepted that Hermogenes reorganized the area at the same time as he rebuilt the temple. We can therefore consider the entire precinct as a unified layout.

Organization of the Site. There is a single entrance through the propylon from the agora. Point A in Figure 95 represents the center of the inner edge of the propylon as determined by Humann's excavations.

SIGHT LINES FROM POINT A

a to left corner of altar of Artemis; left (northwest) corner of temple of Artemis (lowest step); left corner of the raised level for statuary, before the stoas

b to left (northwest) corner of the temple platform (top step, B on the plan)

c to right (southwest) corner of the temple platform (B' on the plan)

d to right corner of the altar of Artemis; right corner of the lowest step of the temple; right corner of the raised level.

ANGLES OF VISION FROM POINT A

Angle $bc = 18° = 180°/10$.

By turning the isosceles triangle ABB' on both AB and AB', we find that points B'' and B''' determine the distance of the north and south stoas from the temple.

DISTANCES FROM POINT A

From point A to the temple façade (AB and AB') — 104.80 m = 300 Ionic feet[2] (34.94 × 300 = 104.80 m).

From point A to the front of the altar of Artemis = AC = 64.70 m.

Hence $AC/AB = 64.70/104.80 = 0.6173 = $ the golden section (0.618).

FIELD OF VISION FROM POINT A

The temple is placed on the center axis of the precinct. Standing at point A, the observer is very conscious of this symmetry. The view is entirely enclosed.

The layout is based on the angle of 18° (180°/10) and the golden section. The entire space of 360° is thus divided into ten parts.

(Notes to this page are on page 155.)

[148]

94   Magnesia, Sacred Precinct of Artemis. View of
site, 1936.

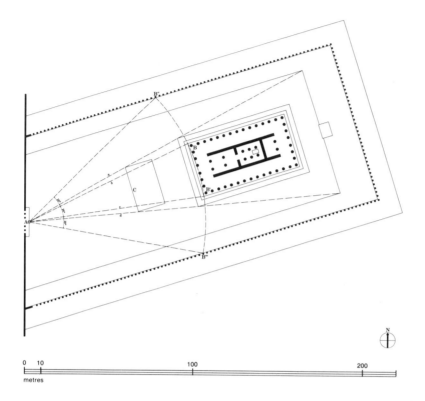

96 Magnesia, Agora and Sacred Precinct of
Artemis. Plan.

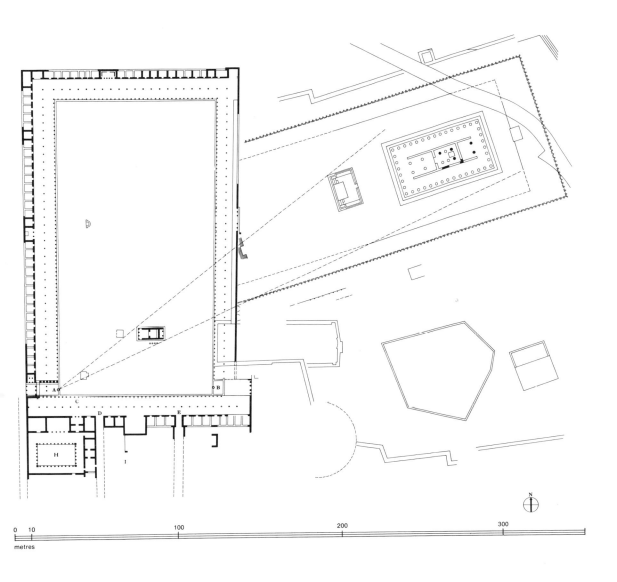

0   10   100   200   300

metres

N

[151]

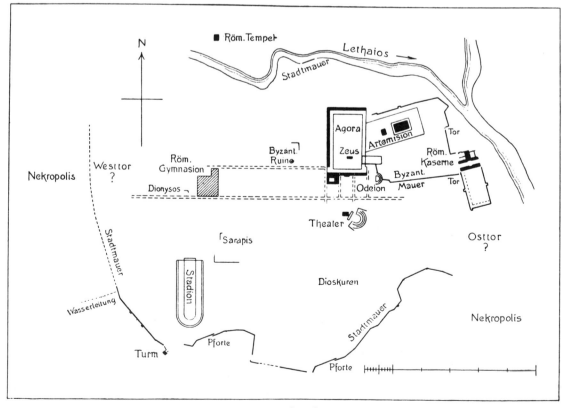

98 Magnesia, Sacred Precinct of Artemis.
Elevations. (Humann.)

99 Magnesia, Sacred Precinct of Artemis.
Perspective of altar and temple of Artemis.
(Humann.)

Halle   Tempel und Altar der Artemis   Halle

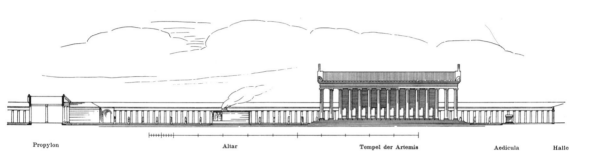

Propylon   Altar   Tempel der Artemis   Aedicula   Halle

The Agora and the Temple of Zeus at Magnesia, Second Century B.C.

Although the agora of Magnesia formed part of the new city plan, prepared about 400 B.C., the small temple that stands within it, the temple of Zeus Sosipolis (Saviour of the City), was not built until the beginning of the second century B.C., possibly after Magnesia's great victory over Miletus. The other buildings, with the exception of a Roman statue to the south of the temple, seem to date also from the second century B.C., and were perhaps built by the architect Hermogenes. The organization of space in the agora can therefore be traced back only to the early second century B.C., and even this cannot be considered definite, as the site has not been completely excavated.[3] It is possible that later findings will give rise to new points of view concerning the layout.

Organization of the Site. The building of the temple of Zeus in the second century B.C. had an important influence on the layout. There are three entrances (Fig. 101). Points A and B are placed in the center of the two entrances east and west of the southern stoa. At a later date two propylaea were built over them. Point C is placed at the access through the southern stoa from the sacred precinct (H in Fig. 96).

The entrances from two roads that lead into the southern stoa from the south, apparently had no influence on the layout of the agora. This seems to be supported by the fact that no attention is paid to the position of these roads in the design of the stoa.

SIGHT LINES FROM POINT A

a to left corner of the propylon of the sacred precinct of Artemis (Figs. 101, 102)

b to left corner of the altar before the temple of Zeus; right corner of the propylon of the sacred precinct of Artemis

c to left corner of the structure in the southwest of the agora; right corner of the altar of Zeus, left (northwest) corner of the temple of Zeus

d to center corner of the southwest structure; right (southeast) corner of the temple of Zeus

e to right corner of the southwest structure.

FIELD OF VISION FROM POINT A

The spectator has an entirely enclosed field of vision in which he perceives each structure in succession, each a complete entity. From left to right (Fig. 102) he sees, without any gaps between them, the propylon of the sacred precinct of Artemis, the altar of Zeus, and the temple of Zeus, with the lower structure containing stone benches in front of it. The position of the temple of Zeus must have been calculated to conceal the larger temple of Artemis, outside the agora (Fig. 95), and thus prevent the competition, in the eyes of the observer, of two equally large volumes.

The position of the southwest structure seems determined by a desire to interrupt the direct view of the Zeus temple, which would otherwise be very dominant, and lead the eye to the path to the altar and, beyond it, to the propylon of the sacred precinct of Artemis.

SIGHT LINES FROM ENTRANCE B

a to left corner of the altar of Zeus (Figs. 101, 103)

b to left (southwest) corner of the temple of Zeus; right corner of the altar of Zeus

c to center (southeast) corner of the temple of Zeus

d to right (northeast) corner of the temple of Zeus; left corner of the exedra opposite the propylon to the precinct of Artemis

e to right corner of the exedra.

SIGHT LINES FROM POINT C

a to left corner of the exedra (Figs. 101, 105)

b to left side corner of the sitting place; right corner of the exedra

c to right corner of the sitting place; left corner of the tall stele

d to right corner of the stele; left corner of the altar of Zeus

e to right corner of the altar of Zeus; left corner of the propylon to the sacred precinct of Artemis

f to left (northwest) corner of the temple of

[154]

Zeus; right corner of the propylon to the sacred precinct of Artemis

g to right (southeast) corner of the temple of Zeus.

Although the space is entirely enclosed, the route to the propylon of the sacred precinct of Artemis is kept entirely clear from each vantage point, with the other structures in the agora ranged on each side of it.

---

[1] Julius Kohte, "Die Bauwerke," in Carl Humann, ed., *Magnesia am Maeander,* p. 163.

[2] [For discussion of ancient Greek feet see Chapter 3, note 4.]

[3] Carl Humann, ed. *Magnesia am Maeander,* p. 107.

Works Consulted by the Author
Gerkan, Armin von. *Der Altar des Artemis-tempels in Magnesia am Mäander.* Berlin: Schoetz, 1929.

Humann, Carl, ed. *Magnesia am Maeander: Bericht über die Ergebnisse der Ausgrabungen der Jahre 1891–1893.* Berlin: Reimer, 1904; in particular, Julius Kohte, "Die Bauwerke," pp. 9–172.

100   Magnesia, Agora. Perspective of temple
of Zeus. (Humann.)

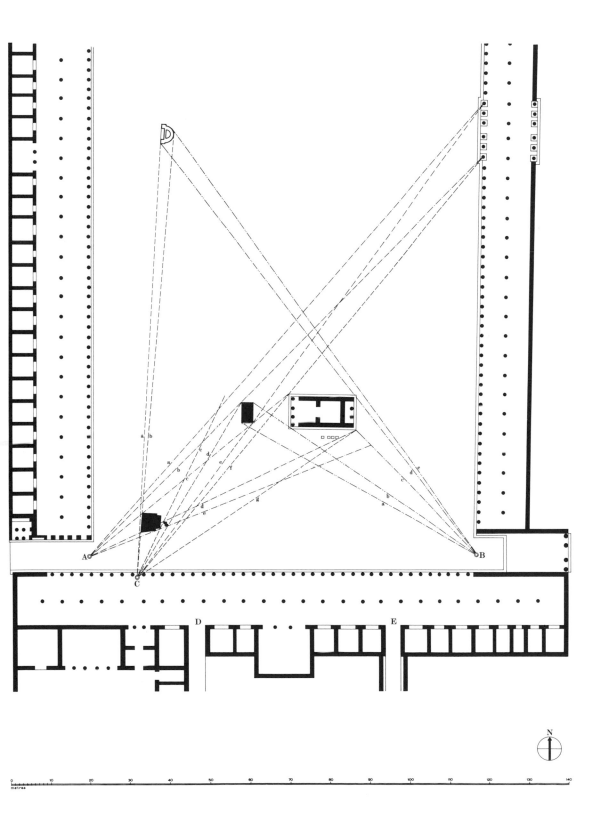

104 Magnesia, Agora. Elevations. (Humann.)

105 Magnesia, Agora. Perspective from point C.

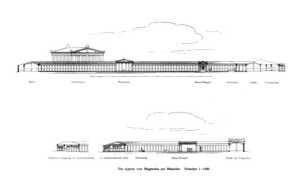

Die Agora von Magnesia am Mäander. Schnitte 1 : 1000.

The Corinthian Temple at Palmyra, First Century A.D.

This precinct was founded in the Roman period, in the first century A.D.[1] It has an axial entrance at A (Fig. 106) and two symmetrical side entrances at M and N. Although the two side entrances seem to have been left open, it was not possible to look from them into the interior of the precinct. Similarly, from inside the precinct, it was not possible to see out through these openings. This is effected by the unusual size and form of the corner columns, which interrupt the view to and from the side openings (see sight lines a, b, a', and b' in Fig. 106). In this way the architect's desire to create a visually enclosed space was maintained.

Organization of the Site. Point A is located on the axis of the central entrance on a line connecting the centers of two columns of the stoa. There is no step.

SIGHT LINES FROM POINT A

c and c' to left and right corners of the temple platform (E and E' on the plan, Fig. 106); left and right far corners of the precinct

d and d' to left and right corners of the beginning of the temple superstructure, i.e., the bases of the nearest columns (B and B' on the plan).

ANGLES OF VISION FROM POINT A

Angle $dd' = 36° = 180°/5$.

DISTANCES FROM POINT A

The distances from point A along lines d and d' to points B and B' are identical and $= 25.5$ m.

The distance from point A to the temple steps (point C'') $= 15.75$ m.

Hence $AC''/AB = 15.75/25.50 = 0.618/1 =$ golden section.

We also find that the distance AC'' is determined by the base of the isosceles triangle ABB':

$BB' = AC'' = 15.75$ m.

The ground plan of the temple platform $EE':E'F = 1:\sqrt{5}$.

The position of the temple is therefore determined by the isosceles triangle ABB' and governed by the 36° angle $= 180°/5$ or the division of the whole field of 360° into ten parts.

[1] I studied the layout of this Corinthian temple precinct from the plans in Theodor Wiegand, ed., *Palmyra: Ergebnisse der Expeditionen von 1907–1917*, 2 vols., Berlin: Keller, 1932. I did not examine the site.

Additional References

Michałowski, Kazimierz. *Palmyre: fouilles polonaises, 1959.* Warsaw, 1960. (This covers only the Diocletian area of Palmyra.)

Schlumberger, Daniel. *La Palmyrène du nord-ouest.* Paris, 1951. (Thesis, University of Paris.)

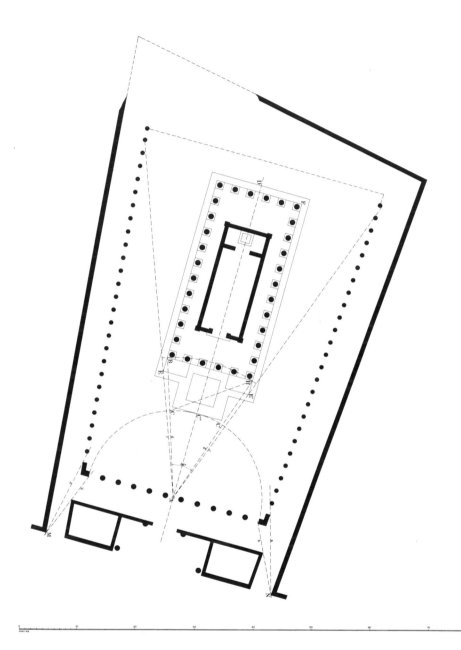

107 Palmyra. Plan of area near east wall of the city. (Wiegand.)

108 Palmyra. Sketch plan of the city. (Wiegand.)

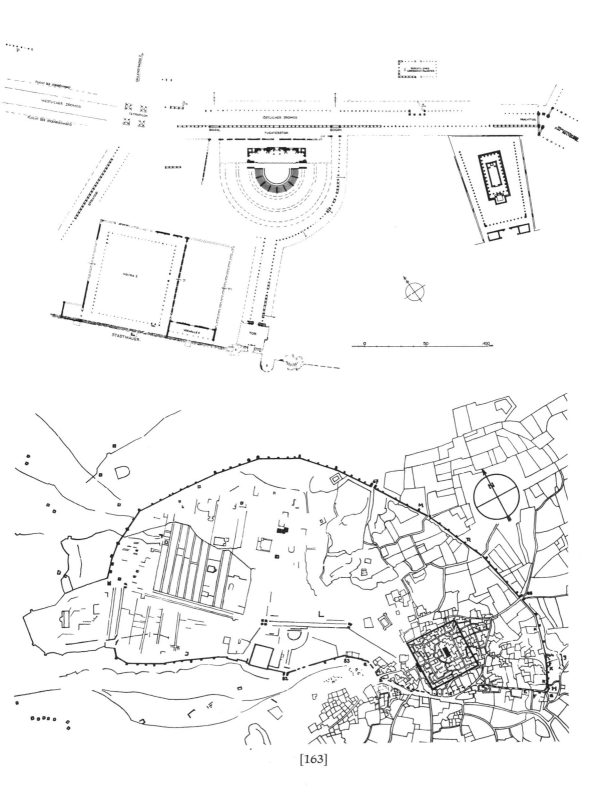

109   Palmyra. View of east end of main street
showing ruins of Corinthian temple in foreground,
circa 1917. (Wiegand.)

110 Palmyra. View showing arch and colonnade
north of Corinthian temple, circa 1917. (Wiegand.)

7 Use of Exceptions to the System

The Sacred Precinct of Demeter Malophoros at Selinus, Sixth Century B.C.

The sacred precinct of Demeter Malophoros is at Gaggera, on the western slope of the river valley, opposite the city hill of Selinus (Fig. 114). The origin of the precinct is uncertain.[1] Koldewey and Puchstein distinguished three important periods of building activity. They attributed the temple, the small altar (between sight lines f and g in Fig. 112), and the votive stele within the propylon to the sixth century B.C.; the propylon to the fourth century B.C.; the three-sided rectangular structure (S in Fig. 112) and the room marked Z on the plan to a much later period.[2] Their opinions must be somewhat revised, however, following the later discovery by Italian archaeologists of the boundary wall and two more buildings to the southwest. As there is no clear picture of the site at any particular period, it seems that the only feasible method is to study the layout as a whole, without reference to the time at which it was planned or completed.

Organization of the Site. The propylon establishes the position of the entrance, and point A lies on its axis midway between the centers of two columns.

SIGHT LINES FROM POINT A

a to left corner of the three-sided rectangular structure (S on the plan)

b to right corner of the rectangular structure (considered by the original excavators to be a "sitting area");[3] left corner of the great altar; left (southeast) corner of the southwestern building

c to left (southeast) corner of the square building to the southwest; right (northwest) corner of the southwestern building

d to left (southeast) corner of the temple; right (northwest) corner of the square building

e to right corner of the great altar; right (northeast) corner of the room marked Z on the plan

f to left corner of the small altar

g to right corner of the small altar.

ANGLES OF VISION FROM POINT A

Angle $ag = 90° = 180°/2$.

From point A the four western buildings can be seen above the altar as a single sequence; no gaps appear between them, and none of them overlaps another.

The path to the megaron passes between sight lines e and f along the open field of vision between the line of structures and the small altar; it leads due west.[4]

---

[1] My studies of this precinct are based on the descriptions in Koldewey and Puchstein, *Die griechischen Tempel in Unteritalien und Sizilien*, and in Hulot and Fougères, *Sélinonte*. I did not examine the site.

[2] Koldewey and Puchstein, *Die griechischen Tempel*, p. 82.

[3] [This rectangular structure has not yet been identified with certainty. It might have served as a podium for sculpture or an altar, or, indeed, it might have been a "sitting area," but the three walls do not look like benches.]

[4] This path was identified by Koldewey and Puchstein (ibid., p. 84).

Works Consulted by the Author

Gábrici, Ettore. "Il Santuario della Malophoros," *Monumenti Antichi* 32, 1927, pp. 6–419.

Hulot, Jean, and Fougères, Gustave. *Sélinonte: La ville, l'acropole et les temples.* Paris, 1910.

Koldewey, Robert, and Puchstein, Otto. *Die griechischen Tempel in Unteritalien und Sicilien.* 2 vols. Berlin, 1899.

Additional References

Santangelo, Maria. *Selinunte.* Translated by G. H. Railsback. Rome, 1953.

White, Donald. "The Post-Classical Cult of Malophoros at Selinus," *American Journal of Archaeology* 71, 1967, pp. 335–352.

111 Selinus, Sacred Precinct of Demeter
Malophoros. Reconstruction from the east.
(Hulot and Fougères.)

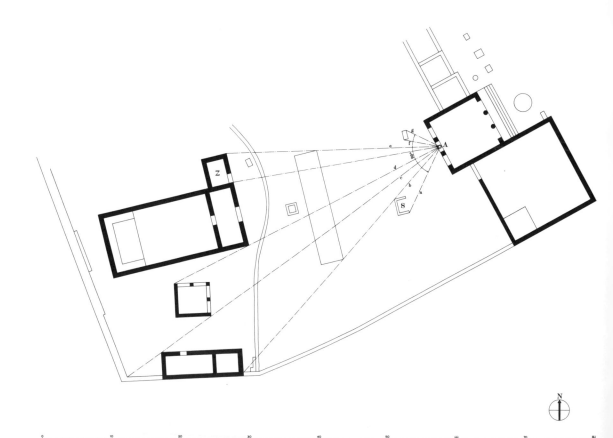

113 Selinus. Sacred Precinct of Demeter
Malophoros. Plan. (Koldewey and Puchstein.)

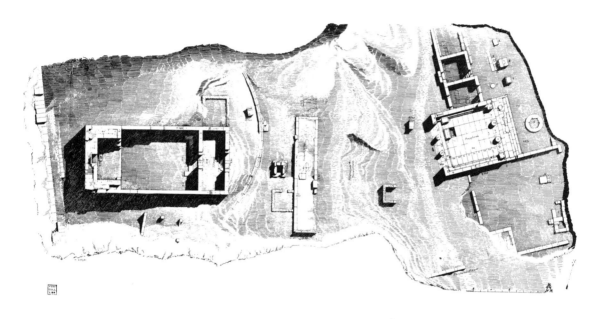

114   Selinus. General plan of the city.
(Hulot and Fougères.)

115 Selinus, Sacred Precinct of Demeter
Malophoros. Plan. (Hulot and Fougères.)

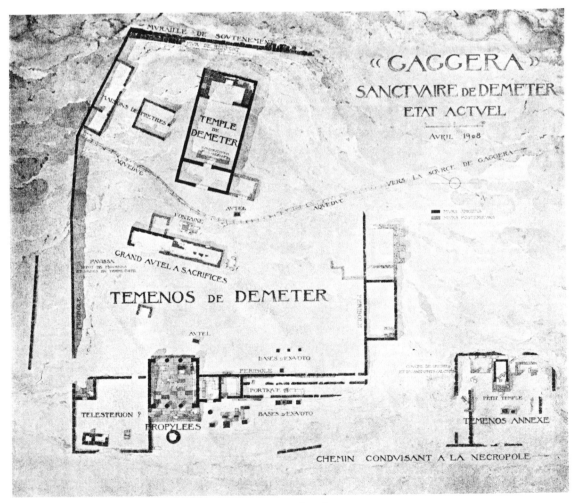

The Sacred Precinct of Athena at Sounion, Fifth Century B.C.

The present condition of the sacred precinct of Athena at Sounion (Fig. 116) permits only an assessment of the layout in the post-Persian period, although we know that even in the time of Homer there existed a holy Sounion.[1] The earliest structure known is a small temple of Athena that was destroyed by the Persians in 480 B.C. The Athenians then built a new, larger temple. The cella was erected first, and a few years later an Ionic colonnade was built round two sides, but both were designed at the same time.[2] It also appears that the earlier small temple of Athena was rebuilt, and it is probable that both temples stood next to one another for a number of years.[3]

It appears that the large altar of Athena was erected at the same time as the new temple, the eastern boundary wall, and the ramp, which shows the position of the entrance to the precinct.[4]

Organization of the Site, 480–450 B.C. The new plan, prepared in 480 B.C. and completed by 450 B.C., paid careful attention to earlier structures (Fig. 117).

One entrance is known; it leads from the ramp at the end of the eastern boundary wall. I have endeavored to identify it as precisely as possible on the site (point A).

SIGHT LINES FROM POINT A

a to left corner of the large altar of Athena (B on the plan, Fig. 117)

b to middle corner of the large altar

c to right corner of the large altar

d to left (southeast) corner of the large temple of Athena

e to right (northeast) corner of the large temple of Athena (C'' on plan); left (southwest) corner of the small temple of Athena

f to right corner of the small, old altar to Athena.

ANGLES OF VISION FROM POINT A

Angle $ad = 30° = 180°/6$.

Angle $de = 90° = 180°/2$.

Angle $ef = 30° = 180°/6$.

FIELD OF VISION FROM POINT A

Standing at point A and looking from left to right, we would see

the large temple of Poseidon on the neighboring hill

a free field of vision

the large altar of Athena

a second, very small, open view

the large temple of Athena

the small temple of Athena

the small altar

It is worth noting that, if the narrow field of vision between the large altar and the large temple (lines c and d) was in fact free, its orientation was almost directly toward the west (10° north of west). It is also striking that the angle of vision between the right corner of the temple of Poseidon and the left corner of the temple of Athena is $60° = 180°/3$. In other words, we find a planned connection not only between the buildings on the site itself but also between important visual elements in the environment.

---

[1] Σούνιον ἱρόν; see Homer *Odyssey* 3.278.
[2] Anastasios K. Orlandos, "Τοῦ ἐν Σουνίῳ ναοῦ τοῦ Ποσειδῶνος τοῖχοι καί ὀροφή," Ἀρχαιολογική Ἐφημερίς, 1917, pp. 213–226; Valerios Stais, "Σουνίου ἀνασκαφαί," Ἀρχαιολογική Ἐφημερίς, 1917, p. 181.
[3] Ibid. Anastasios Orlandos wrote to me that he was certain of this and that he believed both existed until quite a late period.
[4] Stais, "Σουνίου ἀνασκαφαί," p. 181. This is also noted in a letter to me from Orlandos.

116 Sounion, Sacred Precinct of Athena. View
from point A, 1969.

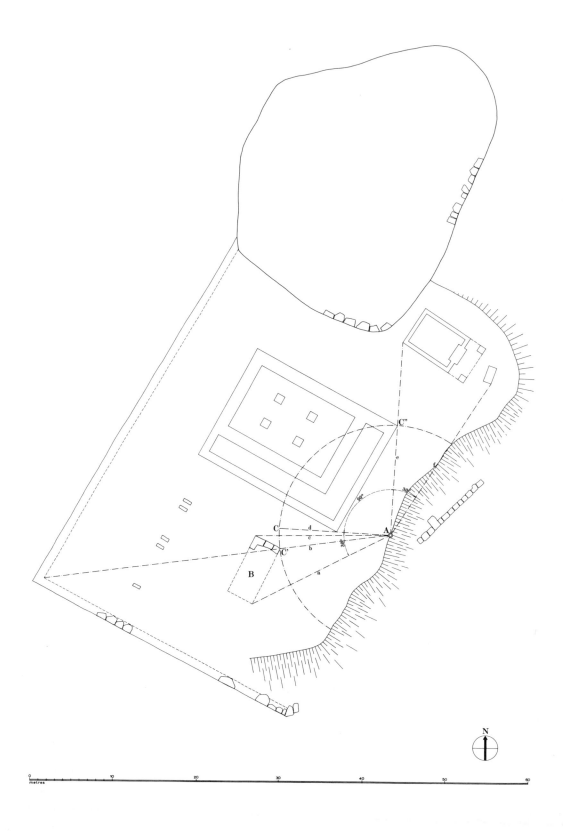

118   Sounion, Sacred Precinct of Athena. Plan. (Staïs.)

119   Sounion. View of temple of Poseidon from the Precinct of Athena, 1969.

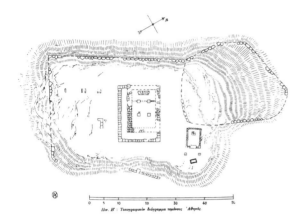

Πιν. Β´ : Τοπογραφικόν διάγραμμα τεμένους ΄Αθηνάς.

The Sacred Precinct of Demeter at Priene, Fourth Century B.C.

The entire layout seems to have been designed and built at the time of the rebuilding of the city in 350 B.C. (Fig. 120). Only the altar (B on the plan) dates from the Roman period.[1]

Organization of the Site, 350 B.C. Point A was taken in the center of the entrance A, on a line with the inner surface of the walls.

SIGHT LINES FROM POINT A

a to right (northwest) corner of the enclosure to the left of the entrance; left (southeast) corner of the temple

b to left (southeast) corner of the temple porch

c to right (northeast) corner of the temple porch

d to left (southwest) corner of the enclosure to the right of the entrance.

ANGLES OF VISION FROM POINT A

Angle $bc = 18° = 180°/10$.

Angle $ad = 36° = 180°/5$.

The frontage of the temple thus occupies half the angle of vision, as in the temple of Zeus at Priene.

When the altar (B on the plan) was built in the Roman era, the existing field of vision was taken into account, and it was located within the only available angle of vision, approximately between lines c and d.

(Notes to this page are on page 178.)

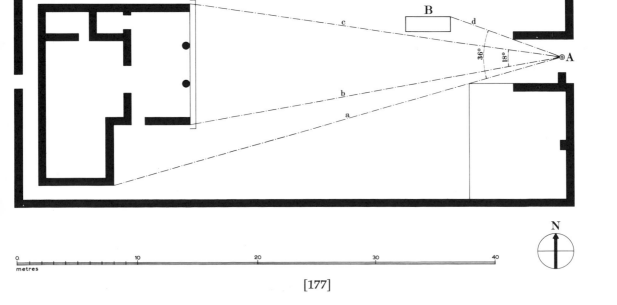

The Sacred Precinct of the Egyptian Gods at Priene, Third Century B.C.

About the middle of the third century B.C., when Ptolemy III of Egypt ruled over Ionia, Egyptian religious cults were introduced into the city of Priene. The first sacred precinct of the Egyptian gods was built during this period (Fig. 121); it was a rectangular courtyard with a propylon (A on the plan) to the east, a great altar in the middle, and perhaps a second entrance in the west wall.[2] Unfortunately, only the foundations of this precinct remain, so that the exact position of the entrances cannot be determined.

Somewhat later, but still in the Hellenistic period, a square propylon (B on the plan) was built in the north wall, and a stoa was erected along the west side of the precinct. This does not necessarily mean that there were formerly entrances at points B and C. It is in fact possible that there was originally only one entrance (A), as in the sacred precinct of Zeus in Priene (Fig. 93).

Organization of the Site. In the first period the main entrance was through the propylon (A on the plan), and it is possible that there were also entrances at B and C.

In the second period the precinct was entered from the propylon A, the propylon B,[3] and the gateway C.

SIGHT LINES FROM POINT A

Point A lies on the axis of the propylon in the center of the oblique line of the propylon frontage, where the door would be.

a to left (southeast) corner of the great altar
b to right (northeast) corner of the great altar.

ANGLES OF VISION FROM POINT A

Angle $ab = 90° = 180°/2$.

SIGHT LINES FROM POINT B

Point B lies on the axis of the propylon along the inner face of the wall.

b to left (northeast) corner of the great altar
c to right (southwest) corner of the great altar
c' to middle (northwest) corner of the great altar.

ANGLES OF VISION FROM POINT B

Angle $bc = 45° = 180°/4$.

Line c' divides this angle equally into two angles of 22.50°.

Hence $180°/8 + 180°/8 = 180°/4$.

SIGHT LINES FROM POINT C

Point C is taken in the center of the entrance on a line with the inner face of the boundary wall.

d to left (northwest) corner of the great altar
e to right (southeast) corner of the great altar.

ANGLES OF VISION FROM POINT C

Angle $de = 44°(45° = 180°/4)$.

FIELD OF VISION

Two major changes occur in the second period. First, the importance of sight line a is enhanced because it leads to the junction of the new western stoa with the south wall of the precinct. Second, the angle between the sight lines from entrance B is no longer 45° but, because the position of point B has moved to B' with the building of the propylon,[4] has become 50°.

It may be added that the angle of 45° (i.e., the division of the total space into eight parts) is encountered nowhere else in Greek layouts. The only other sacred precinct I know of in which it is used is the temple of Isis at Pompeii (Fig. 122), which is also a temple of an Egyptian cult.

---

[1] As in my other studies at Priene, I based my information on Theodor Wiegand and Hans Schrader, *Priene: Ergebnisse der Ausgrabungen und Untersuchungen in den Jahren 1895–1898*, Berlin: Reimer, 1904. I also took measurements on the site.
[2] For this precinct also my information is based on Wiegand and Schrader, *Priene*. In addition, I took measurements on the site.
[3] Wiegand and Schrader, *Priene*, p. 169.
[4] Ibid.

[178]

121 Priene, Sacred Precinct of the Egyptian Gods.
Plan.

122 Pompeii, Sacred Precinct of Isis. Plan.

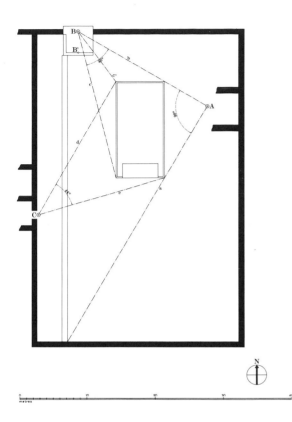

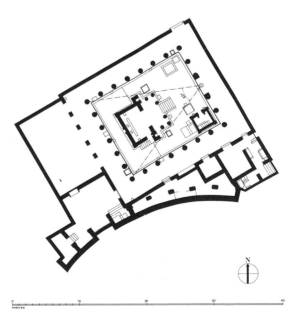

Index

[183]

Sight lines (*continued*)
  at sacred precinct of
    Demeter, Priene, 176
  at sacred precinct of
    Demeter
    Malophoros,
    Selinus, 166
  at sacred precinct of
    Egyptian gods,
    Priene, 178
  at sacred precinct of
    Poseidon, Sounion, 92
  at sacred precinct of
    Olympian Zeus,
    Priene, 146
  at temple terrace of
    Apollo, Delphi, 39
  at temple of Zeus,
    Magnesia, 154
Simplicius, 15
Site planning, 3, 4, 5, 15,
  21, 22
Sounion, sacred precinct
  of Athena, *xxxvi*, 7,
  8, 14, 172, *173*
  plan, *174, 175*
  sacred precinct of
    Poseidon, *xxx, xxxvii*,
    3, 7, 11, 22, 92–93,
    94–95
    plan, *96, 97*
    temple, *xxx, 92–93, 97*
Space, 21
  finite, 15–16
  infinite, 15–16, 21
  organization of, 3, 17,
    20, 23 (*see also*
    Ten-part system;
    Twelve-part system)
Staïs, Valerios, 92
Statues, in site planning,
  20
Stevens, Gorham P., 33
  nn. 6, 9
Stoa, at Acropolis, 29, 30
  at agora, Miletus, 63
  at agora, Priene, 136
  at Altis, Olympia, 71,
    72, 73
  at Asclepeion, Cos,
    125, 126
  at Corinthian temple,
    Palmyra, 161
  at Delphineion,
    Miletus, 54, 56
  at sacred precinct of
    Athena, Pergamon,
    104
  at sacred precinct of
    Poseidon, Sounion,
    92, 93
  at temple of Zeus,
    Magnesia, 154
Sun, view of, 8, 21, 93

Symmetry, 23, 48, 73,
  74, 148

Ten, significance of, 17
Ten-part system, of
  architectural spacing,
  6–8, 9, 12–13
Theocoleon, at Altis,
  Olympia, 72
Theodoros, 21, 114
Theseum (temple of
  Hephaestus),
  Athens, 92
Tholos, at Delphineion
  IV, 56
Triangle, 6; *see also*
  Equilateral triangle
Triglyph, Doric, 19 n. 32
Trophonios, 39
Twelve-part system, of
  architectural spacing,
  6–8, 9, 10–11, 21, 22

Universe, concept of,
  15–16, 21

Victory of the
  Messenians, statue,
  Delphi, 40 n. 4
Victory of Paeonios,
  statue, at Altis,
  Olympia, 72, 73, 74,
  75
View, closed, 8
  open, 8
Viewpoint, 5
  human, 22, 23; *see also*
    Angles of vision;
    Field of vision; Sight
    lines
Visibility, importance
  of, 23
Vision, field of, *see* Field
  of vision
Vitruvius, 15

Wiegand, Theodor, 114,
  146

Zeus, altar of, at
  Acropolis, 31, 32
  altar of, at Altis,
    Olympia, 72
  altar of, Pergamon,
    110, *111, 112, 113*
  sacred precinct of,
    Priene, 3, 6, 7, 13, 22,
    146, 176, 178
  plan, *147*
  temple of, at Altis,
    Olympia, 10, 23,
    71–76
  temple of, Magnesia,
    154–155, *156*
Ziegenaus, Oscar, 116 n. 4

[184]

Delphi •

Athe

Aegina •

Olympia •

Selinus •